THE

BORN

IDENTITY

PHIL PRINGLE

WHO WE ARE
AND
WHAT WE HAVE
IN
CHRIST

The Born Identity by Phil Pringle

Published by PaX Ministries Pty Ltd ABN No: 97 003 162 392
Locked Bag No 8, Dee Why, 2099, Australia
Tel: +61 2 9972 8688 Fax: +61 2 9972 8640
www.philpringle.com

Cover Art and Layout by Sasha White
www.mrandmrswhite.net

Printed and bound at Victory Publishing House
90, P&T Colony, Trimulgherry,
Secunderabad-500 015, INDIA
Email: vph@aol.in

CONTENTS

THE MESSAGE

I called this book 'The Born Identity', playing on the title of the movie of 2006 'The Bourne Identity', when the main character, Jason Bourne, played by Matt Damon, forgets who he is after taking a blow to the head.

Gradually he recovers his skills but his memory is completely blank as to how he came to have those skills and to be in the situation he has found himself in, to be hunted all over the world. He has no idea who is chasing him or why. He scrambles throughout the movie to discover these facts, which remain obscure and patchy in his memory.

Our christian journey is much the same even when we discover who we are in Christ. Often we take 'blows to the head' that dislodge that information leaving us to live in our own strength rather than in the new creation person we have become in Christ.

Paul stated that his central goal was to work hard, even strive, to present every person complete 'in Christ' (Colossians 1:28). He prefaced this by saying his message was Christ Himself, 'Him we preach'. He preached Christ, determining to not know anything else lest it obscure the simplicity and power of the message. Being 'in Christ' is the fulfillment of the entire New Covenant. Once we have this reality at the core of our experience with God, our entire approach to everything is revolutionised. The way and purpose of ministry, of pastoring people, of building the Kingdom and of our own personal walk with God is dramatically adjusted. Outside of Christ we are on our own, naked of power, attempting to accomplish God's work with our strength. Impossible! In Christ we are empowered far beyond our abilities and capacities, super equipped for everything.

Every single person ever born on Earth has been predestined to be born again (Romans 8:29). This has always been the plan of God for every single person. Like the caterpillar that transforms into a butterfly, so every human is destined to be transformed from just being born of earthly parents into also being born of God. However, unlike the caterpillar which has no choice in the matter, the course of nature simply plays out, the creature incapable of doing anything to prevent it, we actually have a choice in whether or not we become 'born of God'. We had no choice in our first birth. We simply just 'arrived'. Our parents made that choice for us. We became infused with a self-aware personality and endowed with freedom of choice. Every inhabitant of Earth is to receive the opportunity to be born again. This is why every believer and every preacher must be engaged in bringing Christ to every person on the planet, so they are able to make that choice, receive Christ and become a child of God. Throughout nature, the process of conception depends on at least two agents being active. In the plant world, bees carry pollen from one part of the plant to the stigma causing fertilisation, thus the plant reproduces itself. We, the church must bring Christ to people so they make the choice to receive Him and are born again.

Billy Graham brought home the truth again and again, simply declaring that people must be born again. He reached countless millions with this message. Many years before him George Whitfield, a contemporary of John Wesley also preached 'You must be born again', relentlessly. He was asked why he always preached the message, 'You must be born again'. Because, he replied, 'You must be born again'. John begins his Gospel revealing how those who receive Christ, receive the power to become children of God. Very early in his writings John records an amazing interaction between Jesus and the religious leader, Nicodemus. The core of Jesus' message to the man is, 'You must be born again'. This was said to a religious man, a good man, a righteous man, a religious leader, a man secretly searching for truth. If this message applies to good, righteous religious people, then it applies to every person in the world. One could easily imagine that being good, or religious, or serving in the church, is enough, but it obviously is not. The man still needed to be born again!

John 3:3 Jesus answered and said to him, "Most assuredly,

I say to you, unless one is born again, he cannot see the kingdom of God."
John 3:4 Nicodemus said to Him, "How can a man be born when he is old? Can he enter a second time into his mother's womb and be born?"
John 3:5 Jesus answered, "Most assuredly, I say to you, unless one is born of water and the Spirit, he cannot enter the kingdom of God.
John 3:6 "That which is born of the flesh is flesh, and that which is born of the Spirit is spirit.
John 3:7 "Do not marvel that I said to you, 'You must be born again.'

The message is utterly clear. Unless we are born again, we cannot 'see or enter' the Kingdom of God. Unless we are born of the Holy Spirit, we are only born of the flesh. It is not an abnormal thing to be born again. It is the plan of God for every single person. All of us have been destined to be born twice. Once, of the flesh, then a second birth, from above, a spiritual birth, of God Himself!

Becoming a Christian is not about becoming religious, joining a particular denomination or subscribing to a belief system. It is about a complete transformation of nature, of motivation, of our reason for living, of our mindset, of our emotional attachments and of our spiritual awareness. It is becoming a 'new species' of person.

(2 Corinthians 5:17)AMP Bible. We receive a new nature, the nature of the Father. This nature comes from our spirit being made alive through connection with God Himself. Sin

disconnects us;

> *Isaiah 59:2 But your iniquities have separated you from your God; And your sins have hidden His face from you, So that He will not hear.*

This separation is finished when we receive Christ as our sacrifice for sin. We are forgiven, cleansed from our sins and so the separation is closed. We become connected with the Father, through which we are born of God by the Holy Spirit.

Our natural genetic coding comes straight from our parents hence we carry the characteristics of our parents, physically, mentally and emotionally. The same applies when we are born of God. We receive the nature of God! The very nature of the Father is created within us. We become like our father in heaven, Jesus becomes our pattern man, 'the firstborn among many brothers' (Romans 8:29).

Since the beginning in the garden of Eden, God has purposed to make man in His image. This begins when we are born again. We become His child. He becomes our Father. We can't pray the Lord's prayer in reality until we are born again. We can't say 'Our Father' when He's not. Only after we have been born of God can we actually cry out, 'Father' (Romans 8:15).

Over the years Hollywood has produced a number of movies employing the 'amnesia' plot, such as 'The Long Kiss Goodnight', 'The Bourne Identity', etc. The theme is that after these people sustained an injury to the head, they then woke up completely unaware of the life they had been living. In both of the above movies the star was previously a highly skilled, assassin or spy. When they find themselves in a fight, their unconscious, automatic responses reveal they've got skills. They discover they can break bones and shoot to kill. They somehow know things they should not.

However, it's not just these latent heroes that are suffering from amnesia. Most believers are living with a permanent kind of amnesia, forgetting who we are. Negative circumstances constantly send us the message that we are far less than what the New Testament declares us to be. Often theology has been twisted to conform to the defeated, negative thinking of people who are interpreting life and God by their circumstances. We need to submit to Scripture, not submit the Scripture to our thinking.

This book is intended to awaken and remind us exactly who we are and what we have. When we enter our battles with a clear knowing of who we are and what we have, we will win.

Another concept that's become widely popular in movies especially of the 'superhero' kind is that when the star has certain clothing on (aka Spiderman, Superman), or when they get inside a special suit (aka Iron Man, Avatar), suddenly they are equipped to do way beyond anything they could ever have achieved on their own. They can fly, destroy whole armies just by lifting their hand, see through walls, use super human strength to pick up buildings, bridges, etc. The amazing thing is that these concepts are not far from Biblical history. Samson lifted the gates of the city, Moses parted an entire ocean with a stick. Elijah prayed a simple prayer and fire scorched the sky. Jesus Himself, walked on water, ascended in the sky, glowed on a mountain, cast out demons and even raised dead people back to life. The New Testament declares we are 'in Him', not just once, but scores of times we are told that our position in life now is 'in' that same person who lived supernaturally on Earth defying the odds on a regular basis. Our 'Avatar', our 'Iron Man' suit is Christ. Living 'in Him', we have skills. We have potential and abilities far beyond anything we could have ever achieved alone. This has always been God's intention that we discover all of who we can be and what we can do, 'in Christ'.

The New Covenant is activated only 'in Christ'. Not by keeping rules, not by attending church, not by being religious, only by being 'in Christ'. The Old Testament demanded that we keep laws that proved impossible to keep. Our flesh confirmed we were incapable of this. However, the New Testament is not about keeping law, but about receiving a new nature through living in Christ. God brought this to us from the Garden of Eden. After Adam and Eve sinned suddenly they became aware they were naked. They attempted to cover themselves with leaves. God supplied them with the skins of animals for clothing. The animals had died as sacrifices for their sins and then their skin was used to clothe them. Our ache to be clothed with another is ancient. This act of God in Eden was a prediction of Jesus being sacrificed for us. Then God clothes us with His 'skin', His life. We are clothed with Him, His righteousness, His glory, His nature. We begin a new way of living, 'in Him'.

In Him I am righteous with His righteousness, not mine.

In Him I have the mind of Christ, the wisdom of God.

In Him I have complete and utter forgiveness, deliverance and healing.

In Him I am completely protected from the attacks of the devil. That the evil one touches me not.

In Him I have total redemption.

In Him I have been transferred from the Kingdom of Darkness to the Kingdom of God's Son. Christ is now my new currency. He is the currency of Heaven. Just as the Australian dollar isn't accepted in European countries, and the Euro isn't accepted in Australia, so my righteousness doesn't work in Heaven. Only Christ's does.

Now Christ is my complete sufficiency for all things. He is the sum of all things.

Jesus Himself introduced this concept;

> *John 15:4 'Abide in Me, and I in you.'*

Paul reveals how this works;

> *Ephesians 3:17 that Christ may dwell in your hearts through faith;*

Christ lives in an environment of faith. Great boldness provides the atmosphere Jesus lives in. Doubt and negativity is not the home of God. In Him is no darkness John says. Not even a shadow of turning. He has declared His Word and will not deviate from it even in the smallest of ways.

Truth is a liberating force. Truth is a person, not a list of beliefs, or a philosophy of thought. Truth is Jesus Himself. We are lost, in darkness and disconnected from God when we are apart from Christ. He is the truth. He sets us free.

Christ liberates us into an entirely new way of living!

As you read this book you'll receive revelation which will become reality.

The revelation of who you are and what you have in Christ becomes the reality of how we do life.

We often view God and Scripture through lenses shaped and colored by our personal experiences. Some people cannot see the Bible as a positive Book. Even the obviously positive portions seem negative to the mind that has been embedded with a grim view of God from early religious influences. I'm believing that these 'grids' will be removed as you read this book and truth enters the deepest part of your mind and spirit, transforming your thinking and motivations, in turn transforming you and your life.

Some people have an inclination towards being negative. There's something wrong with everything, even the good times are bad! They can't see Scripture as positive. Their negative mind darkens every promise.

I want you to let the promises of God dismantle the negative grid you're viewing Scripture through and in your spirit receive the Word, like seed into fertile soil, so it germinates, producing within you a transformation into a New Testament, new creation person.

Truth is sealed in Scripture until the Holy Spirit breaks it open to us. The Book of revelation speaks of 'seals' being broken that had previously concealed what was written within the scrolls. The Bible has entire truths hidden within, until a seal is broken and that particular truth blazes like the midday sun shining from the pages of Scripture. 'Justification by faith', was always contained within Scripture, however, until Martin Luther 'saw' this truth, it remained hidden. Once it was 'out' though, a reformation began which remains the foundation of the entire protestant church, to this day. The Baptism of the Holy Spirit likewise remained hidden from believers until the turn of last century, when the Holy Spirit was poured out in various places around the world. Suddenly it was clearly seen in Scripture as an experience that liberated millions of people into the gifts of the Spirit, empowering the church to become a supernaturally powerful body. Each great new move of God is always accompanied with a corresponding revelation from Scripture, when another 'seal is broken' and powerful spiritual realities are released from Heaven.

When the Word becomes revelation, the church is transformed. As we give ourselves to the Word, its author, the Holy Spirit, illuminates truth to us.

Knowing WHO WE ARE and **WHAT WE HAVE** ushers us into a life lived in New Testament realities.

When we do not know **WHO WE ARE** and **WHAT WE HAVE,** we are unable to enter our land of New Testament promises.

The degree to which we know **WHO WE ARE** and **WHAT WE HAVE** is the degree we enter into what God has prepared for us.

The Israelites baulk at entering the Promised Land because it is infested with giants. They step backwards, away from what seemed impossible to them.

> *Hebrews 3:19 'THEY COULD NOT ENTER IN BECAUSE OF UNBELIEF.'*

God tells them they will die in the desert.

> *Deuteronomy 1:35 'Surely not one of these men of this evil generation shall see that good land of which I swore to give to your fathers,'*

However, God then says that their children, the next generation, **will** possess the land.

> *Deuteronomy 1:39 'moreover your little ones and your children, who you say will be victims, who today have no knowledge of good and evil, they shall go in there; to them I will give it, and they shall possess it.'*

This **'new generation'** is the new creation person we become when we are born again.

This **new nature** possesses the **'new land'** of the **New Testament!**

The 'old nature' wants what the New Testament promises, but it's the 'new nature' alone that can possess them.

All the promises of the New Testament are only relevant to

the BORN AGAIN person. This and all of this alone is what qualifies us to enter into all the New Testament promises for Earth and Heaven, that we are born of God, through the experience of being born again.

The land of Canaan was possessed by a new generation, the children of all those who came out of Egypt. The New Testament promises are possessed by the new man, the new creation person, the person who is born again.

This is revelation knowledge, not head knowledge. We are born again by the Holy Spirit, in our spirit, not **by** the head or **in** our head. Our head doesn't know God. We can know **about** God with our head, but we actually engage and commune with God through our spirit. It's our spirit that **knows** God.

> *John 4:24 God is Spirit, and those who worship Him must worship in spirit and truth.*

> *1 Corinthians 2:11 For what man knows the things of a man except the spirit of the man which is in him? Even so no one knows the things of God except the Spirit of God.*

Our physical body cannot contact God. We can physically feel the presence of God, but this connection originates with our spirit. We can't see Him with our natural eyes, or touch Him physically, or hear Him with our ears, or even taste or smell God with any of our physical senses. Our spirit is the God conscious part of our makeup. Just like our ears don't see light, and our eyes don't hear sounds, so our physical being, which includes our brain doesn't know God. Just as our ears detect, discern and decipher sound, so our spirit is able to know God.

This 'knowing' of God is **light** to our inner man. This is revelation. This is light that enters our spirit. As this 'light' percolates into our mind from our spirit we grasp the truths of God. Truth liberates us. We begin walking in the light, not the dark.

> *John 8:32 And you shall know the truth, and the truth shall make you free."*

As long as we are ignorant of truth we are vulnerable to attack and destruction. The devil works under camouflage.

> *Hosea 4:6 My people are destroyed for lack of knowledge.*

In the parable of the sower and the seed, Jesus reveals that those who fail to 'understand', the word, have the seed snatched from them by the devil.

After the American Civil War (1861-1865), Abraham Lincoln passed legislation that ended slavery and emancipated the captives. However, many of the slave owners ensured that 'their slaves', remained illiterate. They were forbidden to learn reading or writing. There were no books allowed in their cabins. This ensured they would remain ignorant of the fact that they had been set free. In the same way, the devil aims to block revelation knowledge entering our spirit, so that we remain spiritually illiterate. It is this 'knowing' that sets us free from the 'facts' according to the information of our age, and catapults us into New Testament realities. We must learn to walk by the knowledge of revelation in our spirit rather than by what our natural senses tell us.

One method for training elephants in the circus is to chain one of their front legs to a large peg staked in the ground while the animal is still young. When the elephant is fully grown, the trainers no longer need to chain the elephant. They simply put the peg in the ground. The animal thinks it cannot move. The chain is in the elephant's mind. How many of us still think we are chained to the past or other things in our world? The need for us to be transformed in our thinking is enormous.

Revelation knowledge sets us free from the 'pegs' we think we are still chained to.

In the Bible book of Revelation chapter five we read that as soon as the seals of the scroll are broken and the Word unleashed, worship breaks out in Heaven.

Worship of Christ and meditation in the Word are revelation twins. Revelation is the 'revealing' of something previously hidden. Revelation feeds our spirit. The twenty-four elders around the throne fall down worshipping. They cast their crowns before God. All the angels and all the creatures around the throne are in a perpetual wonder of worship. They sing a new song to God. The redeemed sing that God has made them **kings and priests** and they are **reigning in the Earth**. All this follows the Word of God being broken open.

Revelation 6:1... the Lamb OPENED ONE OF THE

SEALS; and I heard one of the four living creatures saying with a voice like thunder, 'Come and see.' And I looked, and behold, a white horse. He who sat on it had a bow; and a crown was given to him, and he went out conquering and to conquer.'

Truth is a river flowing from the throne of God. Walking in this river, one truth leads to another. Truth brings life. Deception brings death. Truth is that tree of life which Adam abandoned in the garden, preferring the tree of knowledge. **Knowledge on its own is not life**. But when knowledge of the Scripture enters our spirit as **revelation, it is life**. It is this '**life**' that heals sickness, casts out demons, and places its possessor in **dominion** on this Earth.

There are two trees in Eden. The tree of life and the tree of knowledge of good and evil. Adam becomes distracted from the unlimited abundance available to him. Temptation draws him to the singular small thing God has forbidden. The devil draws Adam's fascination to the forbidden tree. So, he eats from the tree of death. **He thinks 'knowledge' is preferable to 'life'.**

Accumulating knowledge is not the gaining of 'life'. **LIFE comes from the Word of God.** We receive a 'knowing' in our spirit, rather than knowledge in the mind. The 'tree of **life**' is the Word and the Spirit.

John 6:63 'The words that I speak to you are spirit, and they are life.' - Jesus

All the branches of the Kingdom of God spring from this tree. Salvation, new life, freedom, healing and prosperity flow from this tree.

Every day we get to eat from this tree of life. When we feed on the Word of God, our spirit receives revelation. This is a transforming power, changing us into the image of Christ. Living in the Word of God brings us faith and the power to overcome. It is overcomers who get to eat from this tree.

> *Revelation 2:7 To him who overcomes I will give to eat from the tree of life, which is in the midst of the Paradise of God.'"*

In Matthew 16:18 Jesus says He will build His Church. He says He will build it upon 'this' Rock. That 'Rock' is revelation knowledge. It is supernatural insight about **who Christ is** and **who we are**. Christ knows who He is and what He is meant to do. He says to Peter, '**...you are Peter, and on this rock I will build My church, and the gates of Hades shall not prevail against it.**' Peter needs to become aware of **who he is** and **what he is meant to do** in this life.

He gives Peter clear knowledge of three things.

> **1.** How God has made him, ('blessed are you')
> **2.** How God sees him, (As 'Peter', 'a rock', rather than 'Simon', 'hearing').
> **3.** His destiny. ('Build the church')

In that supernatural moment, Peter awakens to how God

views Him. He begins seeing himself as different to what he had known all his life. His surroundings have told him who he is; an uneducated rough fisherman without any hope for greatness. His occupation, his family, his education, his whole life had produced a grid through which he sees himself. But in a moment Jesus presents him with a prediction, a prophecy giving him an entirely new view. Jesus Christ sees the man totally differently. He doesn't see him as a fisher of fish, He sees him as a fisher of men. He doesn't see Peter as rough, crude, uneducated or locked into an ordinary life. He sees him as a miracle working, Spirit filled, church founding, powerful preacher. Jesus tells Peter he is a rock. An entirely new picture fills his mind. This affects everything! Absolutely everything! Choices about the future. Choices about lifestyle. Suddenly it all changes. **Jesus builds his church on this new creation person.**

A poor self-image undermines anyone's possibilities. The devil knows this. He works ceaselessly at imprinting a poor self-image on the minds of people everywhere. If the devil can get us to doubt who we are, we will be rendered powerless. The most cunning way the devil creates doubt is by using religion! People adopt a small, powerless, weak status. They believe this false humility will please God. However, this is not from heaven. This is a vision from hell. That is exactly how hell wants the people of God to see themselves. We become **cheated out of our inheritance** when we accept this concept about ourselves.

Colossians 2:18 'Let no one cheat you of your reward, taking delight in false humility ...'

Even Jesus was attacked in this area. **'IF you are the Son of God…'** To counter this, the Father gives Jesus something that will empower him to withstand the severest attacks from the devil and the worst circumstances in life.

'YOU ARE my beloved Son'.

Right from the foundation of Christ's ministry, God makes sure His one and only son knows who He is and what He has. He also tells Him He is beloved and that before He carries out any works, great or small, that He, the Father, is pleased in Him.

> *Luke 3:22 … a voice came from heaven which said,*
> *'YOU ARE MY BELOVED SON; IN YOU I AM*
> *WELL PLEASED.'*

Again in the hearing of the three disciples on the mountaintop, the Father declares who Jesus is.

> *Mark 9:7 … a voice came out of the cloud, saying,*
> *'THIS IS MY BELOVED SON. Hear Him!'*

The voice of the Father is so very important to the soul of a son. When a son hears the voice of his father, security quickly follows. It anchors a son's soul. It keeps him on track. God has shown us how as fathers we must keep talking to our sons all the time.

The devil wants Jesus to prove to himself that he is the Son of God, rather than just believe the Word from Heaven, and so tempts him to act in unbelief.

Whatever we act on we strengthen.

If we act on doubt, we strengthen it. We don't actually solve the problem or build our faith. The only way the devil has any chance of gaining access to our lives is through a weakness like doubt. Doubt needs no help to grow, but faith needs reinforcing every day. As we act in faith every day, we reinforce it constantly. When faith strengthens, doubt weakens.

Jesus knows who He is by revelation from the Word. The Holy Spirit 'quickens' makes alive the Word to the Son of God. Every morning God awakens Jesus His Son to fresh truth about Himself.

> *Isaiah 50:4 'He awakens Me morning by morning, he awakens My ear to hear as the learned.'*

Jesus is absolutely clear about his self-image. He knows absolutely He is the Son of God. Time and again He tells others that He is in fact the Messiah, the Son of God, the great I AM. **He gains the knowledge of who He is from the Word of God**, not from a subjective impression or inclination. Every time He says, **'I AM'**, He reveals who He is to the hearers.

> *John 10:9 'I AM the door. If anyone enters by Me, he will be saved, and will go in and out and find pasture.*

Jesus knows He is the way to God. He knows if people connect to Him they will walk through Him, the door, to God. When we know who we are, we behave correctly. We arrange our life properly. We relate to others properly.

> *John 14:6 'Jesus said to him, 'I AM the way, the truth, and*

the life. No one comes to the Father except through Me.'

This is probably the most radical statement of all Scripture. Only a person with the clearest of revelation about who they are can even begin to utter such a thing. Otherwise it is the ravings of an egocentric madman. But this statement is about Jesus. It's about getting people saved. Jesus declares this with the strongest of compassion for a lost world. Revelation about who we are is not just for us, it's for a world needing God. Jesus knows they cannot accomplish this any other way. He alone is the way to God. He alone is the truth of life. He alone is the life that is eternal. This is not about Jesus laying claim to exclusive rights on truth, way and life. This is the Savior of the world desperately laying out reality so those wanting God will know exactly how to get there. If there were others who could be included in the list as the way to God, He will announce them, but there are none. He alone is the Father's choice.

John 6:48 'I AM the bread of life.'

The Bread of life feeds us. This bread satisfies the deepest hunger in the soul of any seeker. This bread feeds our spirit with the finest quality food. Our spirit does not survive without this bread of life, the Word of God. Jesus knows He is that Word, manifested in the Earth. 'Eat Me', He says.

John 15:1 'I AM the true vine, and My Father is the vinedresser.

Again and again, Jesus declares who He is. He relates to the world as He is and His followers in turn relate with Him accordingly. He is the Vine. We are the branches. Therefore we make sure we're connected with Him. Deep, secure, undisturbed and constant.

> *John 6:63 'It is the Spirit WHO gives life; the flesh PROFITS nothing. THE WORDS THAT I SPEAK TO YOU ARE SPIRIT, AND THEY ARE LIFE.*

The Holy Spirit is a person. **'WHO gives life'**.

When we speak the Word of God into any situation the Holy Spirit accompanies our speech. We speak the person of the Holy Spirit into it. WOW!

WHAT LIVES, GROWS!

Life comes from the Spirit.

The flesh cannot give spiritual life. What comes from the flesh fails to grow. The flesh doesn't profit at all (John 6:63)

The Spirit and the Word are what cause 'profit'. In other words, 'blessing' benefit comes from words.

> *James 1:23-25 for if anyone is a hearer of the word and not a doer, he is like a man observing his natural face in a mirror;*
> *24 for he observes himself, goes away, and immediately forgets what kind of man he was.*
> *25 but he who looks into the perfect law of liberty and continues in it, and is not a forgetful hearer but a doer of the work, this one will be blessed in what he does.*

Our problem is;
WE FORGET THE THINGS WE SHOULD REMEM-
BER AND REMEMBER THE THINGS WE SHOULD
FORGET.

> *Isaiah 43:18-19 DO NOT remember the former things,*
> *nor consider the things of old. Behold, I will do a new*
> *thing, now it shall spring forth; shall you not know it?*
> *I will even make a road in the wilderness and rivers in*
> *the desert.*

PRE-OCCUPATION WITH THE PAST PREVENTS US
APPROPRIATING OUR FUTURE.

Why do we look in a mirror?
To see ourselves.

The Word of God is a mirror.
It shows us who we are. The good and the bad.
When we look into the Word we discover what we look like.
Who we are,
What we have,
Where we come from,
Where we are going.
The Word and the Spirit bring revelation. This is what sets
us free. This is how we possess God's promises. We become
aware of who we are according to the Word of God.

IDENTITY
AMNESIA

1. THE PRODIGAL SON FORGETS WHO HE IS

Luke 15:11 … 'A certain man had two sons…'

The younger son knows **what he has** but forgets **who he is**. The older son knows **who he is** but doesn't understand **what he has**.

Children bear the likeness of their parents.

When we are born of God we are His children.

We bear His image in ourselves.

Born of God we carry a resemblance to our Heavenly Father, just as we bear resemblance to our earthly father. We have His characteristics by virtue of the fact that we are born of Him.

We say of people, 'he has his fathers good nature', or, 'she has her father's humor'. Well, we have our Heavenly Father's nature.

The spiritual genetics of God are in the foundation of the born again person. We are not **trying** to be children of God. We either are or we're not. People don't try to be human beings. We are born as such. We would have to try impossibly hard to be a horse because we're not born as horses. But the horse doesn't have to try. He's born a horse. We are born again by the Spirit of God as children of God. We are what God has made us. He has made us in His image.

The prodigal understands what his inheritance is, but doesn't understand his character. He didn't realize who he was. He knows what he has, but not who he is. He is the child of a noble, righteous man. The fruit of his father's life is success and wealth… the blessing of God. **He wants the fruit of his father's life, but not the root of it**. The root is his father's godly God-like character. The fruit from this character is blessing.

He lays claim to his inheritance. However, he squanders it on worthless pursuits because he doesn't realize who he is, and doesn't really want to know. A premature inheritance is always a dangerous proposition.

> *Proverbs 20:21 An inheritance gained hastily at the beginning will not be blessed at the end.*

Our inheritance from God is appropriated step by step so we consolidate our position after each step of possession and victory.

> *Exodus 23:29-30 I will not drive them out from before you in one year, lest the land become desolate and the beast of the field become too numerous for you. 30: Little by little I will drive them out from before you, until you have increased, and you inherit the land.*

Truth doesn't manifest in our lives in one giant moment. We possess our promised land piece by piece. God allows time, warfare and tests so we are established in each piece of the land we possess. We learn to maintain living our lives in the reality of the truth we have appropriated.

> *Philippians 3:16 Nevertheless, to the degree that we have already attained, let us walk by the same rule, let us be of the same mind.*

This includes a walk through the fire. When truth is put through the fire it is welded into our character. Truth is not meant to simply be retained in our minds as information, or even just in our spirit as illumination. **Truth is to become who we are.** We are transformed by truth. Truth becomes grounded in our character as we act on it. When we 'see' the love of God, it never becomes anymore than that unless we activate love in our lives. This appropriates the Word. We will meet opposition as soon as truth enters our inner man. This opposition either strengthens the truth or shakes it out. What can be shaken is shaken and what cannot be shaken is strengthened.

Our level of growth is closely connected to our level of inheritance, meaning that as we demonstrate that we are capable of handling greater blessing, then increased blessing comes into our lives.

> *Galations 4:1-2 Now I say that the heir, as long as he is a child, does not differ at all from a slave, though he is master of all, but is under guardians and stewards until the time appointed by the father.*

The piece of ground we take today is essential for what comes tomorrow. It's the platform for tomorrow's opportunity. If we fail to become grounded in what God reveals to us today, we will be inadequate for tomorrow.

The first trial for the Israelites after leaving Egypt was Marah. After three days without water they became desperately thirsty. Finally they actually found water, but the waters of Marah were sour and undrinkable. They complained. Complaining is the language of victims. When people feel they have no power to change their circumstances they complain. These Hebrews have been slaves for four hundred years. Every morning they awoke to another miserable day of slavery, another day of working incredibly hard for absolutely nothing. They had no power to change anything. Complaining indicates doubt, rather than faith. They are victims of forces stronger than themselves. God delivers us from Egypt so we are transformed from victims to victors, from the powerless to the empowered, from slaves to masters. We meet with trials that are designed to arouse the image of God within. Sometimes it's only in a fight when we discover we have the skills to win. The wilderness is our learning center. Even though God provided for His people in the desert by His own sovereign power, He never intended it to continue that way. He wanted His people to discover that they themselves could overcome their enemies, create farms, build cities and nations. We possess our Canaan when we know that **we** are overcomers of giants. In fact God won't destroy them for us. **God moves in our moving.** When we fight, so does He. He accompanies us, not to do it all for us, rather to empower us and work with us. Instead of complaining at the waters of Marah, we address the problem and make changes. Moses hears from God. 'Throw a tree into the waters.' It seems unusual, but he obeys. He throws a tree into the waters. They are healed. The people drink. Problem solved! We act, God moves.

This is how we grow. We don't remain slaves. We change. We become rulers in life. We possess our New Testament inheritance.

The prodigal son shamed his family, living a wild, unrestrained life. His money ran out. He is left without any friends. The only job he could find was feeding swine in a stranger's field in a strange land.

After a time he finally 'awakened'. He '**comes to himself**'. He remembered **who he really was**. He humbled himself and began the return to his father's house. He walked the long pathway home. As he neared the house, the father ran to him. The startled boy feared his father was going to produce a shotgun and start firing, telling him to get off the property and never return. But exactly the opposite happened. The father hugged and kissed his returning son.

God watches for all of us every day, just like the father in this story, waiting, fully expecting our return home. He doesn't condemn those returning. He has a calf ready for the party. He's planned for when we return. He sees us coming back! Every day, He's ready for the homecoming party.

The prodigal planned to plead to be received back into the house as just a servant. However, he never even gets to make this request. Before he can say anything the father has fully welcomed him home. He declares he is his son and will accept him in no other way.

> *Galatians 4:7 Therefore you are no longer a slave but a son, and if a son, then an heir of God through Christ.*

Because he was the father's son, the family ring was placed on his finger, a robe on his back, shoes on his feet. Then the father called all his neighbors and friends of the young man and they had a 'fatted calf' party. This is the love of God. The father didn't tell the boy to go out, work on the farm and earn his way back into favor. No, he immediately gave him all the rights and privileges of a son. This is 'grace' unmerited favor not 'works'. We are the recipients of unearned blessings, given to us in spite of however bad we have been. In Christ we receive all that God has given to Jesus Himself.

THE BEST ROBE

The best robe is Christ's righteousness. It is a gift. Freely given. This is our salvation. We stand before God in perfect, unspotted righteousness. For the son to put the best robe on, his filthy garments needed to be shed. This was no ordinary robe. It was the best in the house. He was received as a son, not a servant or slave. From the beginning, when Adam and Eve made the first sinful blunder, God clothed them with the skins of animals, replacing the fig leaf covering of their own making. If animal skins are the clothing for Adam and Eve, obviously animals have died. This was God atoning for the sins of Adam. Sin demands death. This was the first sacrifice, predicting the death of Jesus many centuries later, for our sins. Yet it was the skin of the sacrificed animals that gave them clothing. In the same sense we are clothed with Jesus' skin. His perfect life becomes ours when we receive Him as our Saviour.

THE RING

The ring for his finger gave the boy the same authority as the father. In Gen 41:42 Pharaoh, the King of Egypt, gave his ring to Joseph. From that point on he had the same authority as the King. Joseph gave orders as though they were from the King himself. Once the boy received such a ring he could punch it into a clay tablet at any place of business and it was like a credit card. It would be accepted as payment. It could be used to transact legal documents. It could be used to establish rights and privileges in political affairs and authority with government officials. We are given the name of Jesus immediately we return to the House. It is His authority given to us, neither earned nor merited. It's our sign of belonging to the royal family of God. Matthew 28:18 tells us that Jesus has been given all authority in heaven and Earth. In turn, He has transmitted this authority to us, to you and I who believe in Him.

SANDALS

Only slaves went barefoot, without sandals. This boy is no slave, but a son, straight away. He's given sandals for his feet, meaning he was barefoot, showing he had become extremely poor, because the sandal was the most basic of clothing. It protected the wearer from all the dirt and faeces of animals that collected on the sandals of walkers. Thus they were never worn inside a house... God gives us sandals to lift us above the level of the unshod servant to the status of sons. In the Old Testament, Moses was told to remove his sandals in the presence of God. Here in the New Testament sandals are fitted on our feet because we have the standing of Christ in the New Testament. Under the Old Covenant people could only stand on their own righteousness and that was not enough, even for a holy man such as Moses. We stand before God, 'in' Christ, not in our works. Astonishingly, we have been granted the same standing before God as Jesus Himself, seated with Him at the right hand of the throne of God.

The utter generosity and high abundance of God's grace is difficult to comprehend. God is amazing! He responds not to our efforts but to His own heart of love for us. He is moved by His own nature of grace and generosity towards sinners. This is God's glory, His grace, manifested in unqualified, generous abundance.

2. THE ISRAELITES AT CANAAN FORGET WHO THEY ARE

Numbers 13:33 'There we saw the giants … AND WE WERE LIKE GRASSHOPPERS IN OUR OWN SIGHT, and so we were in their sight.'

The Israelites finally passed through the desert and arrived at the border of their promised land, Canaan. At the request of the people Moses sent spies into the unknown territory. The mission of these spies was to find a way into Canaan, where Israel could both pitch their tents and begin their conquest.

The spies returned with glowing reports about the land. But they also had bad news. They said it was impossible to take possession of the land because of gigantic warriors who occupied Canaan. All the people became terrified. They turned back. They refused to go in.

When the spies saw the giants, they saw themselves how the giants saw them... AS GRASSHOPPERS. They **forgot what manner of people they were**. God had performed countless miracles for them, including parting the Red Sea and delivering them from slavery, yet facing giants, they didn't believe that either God or themselves could be victorious battling these inhabitants.

The book of Hebrews says in Chapter Ten they **'shrink back to destruction'**. They diminished in size. They moved backwards. They moved towards destruction, all because they refused to move forward in faith. Moving in faith is to move forwards. Moving in faith is to get bigger. We move towards the fulfillment of God's promises, our land of promise.

Those who allowed fear to rule them perished in the wilderness. The spies were chosen because they were leaders of every tribe. When they returned with the negative report, they all fell down dead after bringing the bad news. They discouraged the spirit of God's people. They stopped them entering God's plan. God's displeasure is not unclear! He loves faith. He hates unbelief.

If we are a leader of any kind in the Kingdom of God **it is imperative we create faith, not fear** in our people. Ministers perish in their ministry when they preach doubt instead of faith. The only leaders who survived that day were Joshua and Caleb. They both stood alone in their opposition to the multitude of doubters. They believed God. They told the great congregation that the giants were **'bread for us'**. They said, let's go up at once and possess the land. These two survived a forty-year detour in the wilderness. Eventually Joshua became the leader of the entire nation. He succeeded Moses, leading the Israelites into their promised land.

The sobering fact here is that if we are not living a life of faith, we are unprepared for the moment when faith must be summoned to take advantage of an opportunity. Sadly, the opportunity to enter Canaan was going to last just one day. The unbelieving Israelites were in remorse the next morning, grinding their teeth as they realized they had done the wrong thing. So they told Moses they would go up and possess the land. Surely this would put things right. However, Moses told them that that opportunity was yesterday. Today was the beginning of a forty-year walk in the wilderness. They ignored Moses and attempted to enter their promised land. They were horribly unsuccessful. The Amorites chased them like 'hornets' (Deuteronomy 1:44) There are times and seasons that God has ordained. Obedience always requires faith. Keeping ourselves in faith means we will be ready and able to obey when the moment arrives.

Joshua and Caleb **did not forget who they were** under pressure. They knew they were the people of God. God would give victory. The rest of the congregation **forgot who they were** and perished in the wilderness.

God did not tell them they were **going to** possess the land. He told them He **had already given** the land to them. It was theirs for the taking. As far as God was concerned they already had the land. He had given it to them, past tense! Even the Canaanites knew God had given the Israelites their land. They were in fortress mode, bolting doors and gates, terrified of the approaching Israelites and their God.

Joshua 6:1 Now Jericho was securely shut up because of the children of Israel; none went out, and none came in.

Canaan, apart from being a paradise piece of real estate was also a metaphor for 'rest'. After four hundred years of having no land to call their own, this would be finally their own land, so they could settle. They could rest. This 'rest' does not accidentally happen to us. We need to do whatever it takes to 'enter' this place we own. This 'rest' is New Testament living according to Hebrews. It is the 'rest' of God. When God created the heavens and the Earth, He rested on the seventh day. This is the rest we enter. He does not rest because He is tired. He rests because He has **finished.** In the same way Christ has finished providing salvation. He cried from the cross, **'It is finished'.** Man was created on the sixth day, the day before the seventh. His first day of life was a day of rest, a day in fellowship with God. This is what God wants more than anything else. Life with God is meant to be easy and enjoyable. Religiosity wants us to work hard to try and please God rather than rest, fellowship and please Him. We are to work from a place of rest, secure that we are already accepted with the father, not trying to gain that acceptance with him.

3. GIDEON FORGETS WHO HE IS

Gideon remembers who God is. He remembers God's acts. However, he has forgotten, who he himself is. He has passion, but no faith in who he is as a covenant child of God.

Judges 6:12-13 And the Angel of the LORD appeared to him, and said to him, 'The LORD is with you, you mighty man of valor!'
13: Gideon said to Him, 'O my lord, if the LORD is with us, why then has all this happened to us? And where are all His miracles, which our fathers told us about, saying, 'Did not the LORD bring us up from Egypt?' But now the LORD has forsaken us and delivered us into the hands of the Midianites.'

The Lord calls Gideon a mighty man of great courage, yet he is hiding in a wine press trying to thresh wheat. He is hiding from the Midianites who are regularly attacking Israel, destroying all their crops, keeping them poor. Gideon's reply to the angel is that basically he is a 'nobody'.

Judges 6:15 So he said to Him, 'O my Lord, how can I save Israel? Indeed my clan is the weakest in Manasseh, and I am the least in my father's house.'

He said his clan was the weakest, his family was hopeless and he was the most hopeless in his hopeless family. God persisted with this negative man. He got him through all his self-doubt. Eventually Gideon actually does deliver Israel from their oppressors. He did everything he didn't believe he could do. Every step of this journey Gideon doubts who he was and what he has got. He doubted it was God who was speaking to him, so he put out 'fleeces' to gain proof it was God. He doubted that he would be victorious, so God arranged for him to hear the dream of an enemy soldier. In the dream Gideon won the battle. He doubted he would win the battle because his army was too small. He had about thirty two thousand soldiers. So God proceeded to make his army, not bigger, but smaller, twice, till it was only three hundred strong.

Our answer is always in God, who is with us. He can do the impossible through who we are and with whatever we have got. He works with us just as we are. He works with what He has placed within us, even when we have difficulty recognizing it. And the beautiful part of this is that what we have is ALL that the New Testament promises. Who we are is a NEW CREATION PEOPLE CREATED IN THE IMAGE OF GOD.

On the other hand, Joseph did not forget who he was. As a teenager he saw the vision of who he was going to become. He would be a king, with people bowing down to him. He saw himself on a throne. However, when he told his brothers how he saw himself, they despised him, so much so that, they decided to kill him. They threw him down a pit. However, when some slave traders came by, they decided to sell their brother into slavery. We could be forgiven for imagining this would cause Joseph to become very negative, downcast, walking with sagging shoulders, bent over and glum. But no, he walked like he saw himself, a king. He would not let his circumstances make him forget who he was. He walked like a king. He was purchased as a slave. Did he walk around his owner's house like a poor, intimidated slave? No, he walked like a king. He rose within the household to become the overseer of all the wealthy man's possessions. Because he did not forget who he was, he was blessed in all he did. The household of Potiphar prospered. But then he was accused of the attempted rape of his owner's wife. Without a fair trial, he was thrown into prison. Once again, he could easily have adopted the negative thinking, the downcast attitude and the posture of defeat, walking with sagging shoulders and the swag of a victim. But, he didn't. He walked according to the vision he had of his future rather than the memories of his past. He walked like a victor, not a victim. He walked like a king. He rose to become the guard of the entire prison. All that he oversaw prospered. Because he refused to forget who he was, he was blessed in what he did. Eventually he is summoned to interpret the dream of the Pharoah, because no one else can. He does so, plus he offers wise advice for the national economy that causes Egypt to become one of the wealthiest and most powerful nations of its time. In a single day Joseph was elevated to sit with the King as the Prime Minister of the Nation. His circumstances had eventually conformed to the way he saw himself. He refused to forget who he was.

REVELATION KNOWLEDGE

John 13:1-4 Now before the feast of the Passover, when Jesus knew that His hour had come that He should depart from this world to the Father, having loved His own who were in the world, He loved them to the end. And supper being ended, the devil having already put it into the heart of Judas Iscariot, Simon's son, to betray Him, Jesus, knowing that the Father had given all things into His hands, and that He had come from God and was going to God, rose from supper and laid aside His garments, took a towel and girded Himself.

Revelation is 'knowing' things from the Word and the Holy Spirit

These are things we 'know' deep in our spirit, rather than in our mind.

This is when truth becomes more than just information. It becomes something we had never realised before. We 'see the light'

When information becomes revelation.

When communication becomes transformation.

When data becomes faith.

1 Corinthians 2:12 Now we have received, not the spirit of the world, but the Spirit who is from God, that we might KNOW the things that have been freely given to us by God.

The Holy Spirit has been given to us so we 'know' all that God has freely given to us, and all the plans He has for us and the strategies to achieve those plans.

Jesus KNOWS four things at this moment in His life.

1. **Timing** - He **knows his hour** has come and he is about to depart. He knows and accepts the timing of God.
2. **Authority** - He knows the Father has given all things into His hands.
3. **Standing** - He knows He has come from God.
4. **Purpose** - He knows He is going to God.

1. HE KNOWS HIS HOUR HAS COME

Better to know our hour is coming than to find out it has been. When we know our future we prepare for it. Otherwise, we meet it unprepared.

All of us have 'moments' in our lives when certain things happen. The purposes of God come down to a moment, a day, an hour. It's imperative we recognize those 'moments'. We cannot organize these 'times', we simply recognize them. They are in the Father's hands. Once we have recognized them, we must seize them.

HE 'KNEW' THE FATHER HAD PUT ALL THINGS INTO HIS HANDS.

What do we have from the Father?
What do we have in our hand?

> *Exodus 4:2 So the LORD said to him, 'WHAT IS THAT IN YOUR HAND?' And he said, 'A rod.'*

II Kings 4:2 So Elisha said to her, 'What shall I do for you? Tell me, WHAT DO YOU HAVE IN THE HOUSE?' And she said, 'Your maidservant has nothing in the house but a jar of oil.'

What HAS God put into your hands?

The tense is important. God already **HAS given us things**. We are **not trying to get** these things. **They are already in our hands.** We may not be able to see them, touch them, taste them or feel them, but **they are more real than the Earth we stand on**. These are eternal things that last forever.

The Earth will pass away.

The Word will never pass away.

The truth is we have them now.

The **facts** will rarely tell you this.

The facts are...., but, the truth is...!

The facts may be you're sick, BUT, the truth is, you're healed.

The facts may be you're poor, BUT, the truth is, you're prospering.

The facts may be things are going bad, BUT, the truth is, 'everything is working together for good'!

It's a case of possessing the truth so it becomes a reality.

It is a matter of **revealing reality**.

It is a case of the manifestation of a reality not seen by the natural man, but believed by the spiritual man.

God speaks in **past tense** when he is bringing us into His promises.

God's past is our future.

He lives at the end of time.

He looks back on what is yet to happen in our life.

He looks back on our future!

When we believe what He says, we enter into agreement with God.

We walk with God.

We receive imputed righteousness just as Abraham did when he believed an impossible thing had already happened.

> *Romans 4:17 (as it is written, 'I HAVE MADE YOU a father of many nations'. ... God, who ... calls THOSE THINGS WHICH DO NOT EXIST AS THOUGH THEY DID;*

> *Joshua 1:3 'Every place that the sole of your foot will tread upon I HAVE GIVEN YOU, as I said to Moses.*

> *John 11:41 Then they took away the stone from the place where the dead man was lying. And Jesus lifted up His eyes and said, 'Father, I THANK YOU THAT YOU HAVE HEARD ME.*

> *1 Corinthians 15:25 For He must reign till He has put all enemies under His feet.*
> *... For 'HE HAS PUT ALL THINGS UNDER HIS FEET.'*

> *Joshua 10:8 And the LORD said to Joshua, 'Do not fear them, for I HAVE DELIVERED THEM into your hand; not a man of them shall stand before you.'*

Judges 7:9 It happened on the same night that the LORD said to him, 'Arise, go down against the camp, for I HAVE DELIVERED IT INTO YOUR HAND.

2. JESUS KNOWS HE HAS COME FROM GOD

What does my past look like? Doesn't matter! No matter what your past looks like, once you are born again you have changed family trees. You are now descending from the family tree of God Himself. You have become a brother or sister of Jesus Christ. He is the firstborn among many brethren. You are amongst those who are his 'brethren'. Our old nature came from Adam. We therefore came under the dominion of the devil. Once we have received Christ into our lives we switch rulers. We come under the authority of our Father in Heaven, which in turn means we come under the authority of Jesus Christ. He rules our lives. When we look back at our lives, our sins are forgiven. Our entire sinful nature is wiped out. Our old nature inherited from Adam is destroyed through union with Christ. This is where we are coming from.

When we accept that God has placed all that the New Testament promises in us already, we have begun to agree with God. We align ourselves with Him in eternity, beyond time, once we believe realities not yet seen. Just because we do not physically experience a truth in Scripture, that does not mean it is not real. This is what faith is. **We do not need faith for what we cannot see. We need faith for those things we are unable to see, taste, smell, touch or hear.** This is what New Testament reality is. Believing what is invisible to the natural eye. Even though we are forgiven, there are times we will doubt that. Nevertheless the fact remains, if we have received Christ we are still forgiven whether we feel it or not. In exactly the same way, we are healed, we are prosperous. **We are whatever the New Testament says we are, no matter what our physical senses are trying to tell us.**

Paul seeks to enlighten the Corinthians about what they have not realised – 'Do you not know…?'

> *1 Corinthians 6:9 Do you not know that the unrighteous will not inherit the kingdom of God? Do not be deceived. Neither fornicators, nor idolaters, nor adulterers, nor homosexuals, nor sodomites,*
> *10 nor thieves, nor covetous, nor drunkards, nor revilers, nor extortioners will inherit the kingdom of God.*
> *11 And SUCH WERE SOME OF YOU. BUT YOU WERE WASHED, BUT YOU WERE SANCTIFIED, BUT YOU WERE JUSTIFIED IN THE NAME OF THE LORD JESUS and by the Spirit of our God.*

3. WHAT DOES OUR PRESENT LOOK LIKE?

Our present state is that we are full children of God. This is not something we are going to become in the future. It is a current, present fact!

> *I John 3:2 Beloved, NOW we are children of God*

No one is a complete person until they are in Christ. We were created to be fulfilled in Christ, nowhere else. Our hearts and souls will always be missing the most essential ingredient until we receive Jesus, but when we receive Him, then we are complete in Him.

> *Colossians 2:9- For in Him dwells all the fullness of the Godhead bodily;*
> *... and YOU ARE COMPLETE in Him, who is the head of all principality and power.*

The word 'complete' is very powerful. Brown/ Driver/ Briggs define this Greek word, *pleroo,* as;

to make full, to fill up, that is, to fill to the full, to cause to abound, to furnish or supply liberally; 'I abound, I am liberally supplied'.

to render full, that is, to complete

to fill to the top: so that nothing shall be wanting to full measure, to fill to the brim

to consummate (a number)

to make complete in every particular, to render perfect

to carry through to the end, to accomplish, to carry out, (some undertaking)

to carry into effect, to bring to realization, to realize

used of matters of duty: to perform, to execute

used of sayings, promises, prophecies, to bring to pass, to ratify, to accomplish

used to fulfill, that is, to cause God's will (as made known in the law. to be obeyed as it should be, and God's promises given through the prophets, to receive fulfillment)

Because in Him dwells all the fullness of the Godhead, we therefore are COMPLETE in Him. It is impossible to receive any more than we already have. When we received Christ we received the fullness of the Godhead.

The Todays Living Bible version translates this magnificently;

> *Colossians 2:9-10 For in Christ there is all of God in a human body;*
> *so YOU HAVE EVERYTHING WHEN YOU HAVE CHRIST, and YOU ARE FILLED WITH GOD through your union with Christ. He is the highest Ruler, with authority over every other power.*

Paul urges the Colossian Christians to remain **in Christ alone** and not add to what He has achieved through adding any other efforts of their own. There is nothing we can add to the salvation Jesus has secured for us. It is a complete work. It is a perfect work. It is an absolutely all sufficient work.

He tells them they were **cheated through empty philosophy and vain deceptions** which removed them from a 'Christ only' focused life.

In Christ dwells all the fullness of the Godhead bodily. The God presented between the cherubim, as a cloud over Israel, and as a fire in the night - this same God now dwelt in Christ, not as in a figure or a shadow or a type, but in the actual body of Jesus Christ. And now that same Christ, the risen Christ dwells in us, also not as a metaphor or virtual symbol, but in actual reality.

> *John 1:16 And of His fullness we have all received, and grace for grace.*

4. HE KNOWS HE IS GOING TO GOD

What does my future look like?

We all have a personal destiny. This is tied into our gifts and calling. Whatever your purpose is, God has gifted you to accomplish it. God doesn't tease us with a purpose which we are ill equipped to perform. God has given us the abilities to accomplish anything and everything He has called us to do. He has arranged your life so His purpose will be fulfilled. There is a grand destiny every one of us is called to. This is the ultimate intention of the Father. Even though our specific calling is obviously very important, still the highest point of our calling is for us to be conformed to **the image of Christ.**

> *Romans 8:29 For whom He foreknew, HE ALSO PREDESTINED TO BE CONFORMED TO THE IMAGE OF HIS SON, THAT HE MIGHT BE THE FIRSTBORN AMONG MANY BRETHREN.*

We are conformed to the image of Jesus Christ by the transforming power of the Holy Spirit. **Jesus is the pattern man**. Our character is to reflect His. All of us are to be that unique person that God has designed us to be, yet we are also founded on the nature and character of Jesus Himself. He is the new Adam. He is the progenitor of a whole new race of people. Jesus is the **'only begotten'** of the Father. We are **created** anew in the image of God. Jesus was born of a woman and begotten by God. We are **conformed** by the power of the Holy Spirit to the image of Christ, who was **born in the flesh** by the power of the Holy Spirit. We are **born again** by the power of the same Holy Spirit.

This is why we must remain Christ centred. Our vision is to remain clearly focused on Christ. He fills our view. We abide in Him and He in us. The Holy Spirit changes us into that image. With Jesus in full view we are changed into that same image through the power of the Holy Spirit within.

> *I John 3:2... and it has not yet been revealed what we shall be, but we know that when He is revealed, we shall be like Him, for we shall see Him as He is.*

5. WHO ARE WE?

The Apostle Paul tells us we are **God's workmanship** - Ephesians 2:10..

Vines expository Dictionary of New Testament Words tells us this is where the English word 'poem' comes from. It means something that is 'made'. We are God's creations. The Creator has created. Human beings are His highest act of creation. We are His masterpiece. He took clay and made a masterpiece. The devil, thrown out of heaven and rejected forever by the Creator despises all that He has made, especially those that bear the same image. The devil is relentless in seeking to destroy the image of God in the Earth. Sickness, sin, rebellion, tragedy, anything that will kill, steal or destroy this masterpiece is the malicious purpose of the prince of darkness. The arch enemy of the great artist has trespassed into the gallery. He has attacked it with his deadly forms of graffiti, bats, knives, fire, anything to destroy the work of the artist.

When it was decided to clean and restore the ceiling of the

Sistine Chapel in the Vatican at Rome, amazing discoveries were made.

For centuries art historians had concluded that Michelangelo employed subdued colors because that was what God is like - muted, darkish, colourless. Yet as the restoration began, it became obvious he had actually used some of the brightest colors imaginable. The smoke, wax and grime from the candles plus some bad varnishings over the centuries had discolored the original. Incredible! People had developed opinions about God and the artist with complete ignorance of reality. Only as the restoration began did the artist's view of God become clear. The *Times'* art critic Rachel Campbell-Johnston, says, *'Michelangelo is being reassessed. Every book on this artist will have to be rewritten declare historians who marvel at the newly revealed drama of vivid colour.'*

The 'smoke' of religion over the centuries has deeply blurred, darkened and discoloured the view people have of the Father in Heaven. They come to imagine Him as dark, subdued, muted and somber, just like His representations. Yet, when a restorer comes, the colours of God are radically altered. We see God as He is, and therefore also see ourselves as we are meant to.

After we join with Christ He begins the restoration. What is the model to guide us as to what we are ultimately going to look like? Jesus! He is the restoration template. He is our restoration complete.

> *I John 4:17 ... AS HE IS, SO ARE WE IN THIS WORLD.*

He heals the sick, He defeats the tempter, He walks on the water, He commands the winds and waves, He raises the dead, He makes disciples, He brings salvation, He multiplies the food, He brings blessing to people, He brings forgiveness and mercy. That's the image we are being changed into.

WE ARE THE IMAGE OF GOD IN THE EARTH

Genesis 1:27 So God created man in His own image; in the image of God He created him; male and female He created them.

Created - naseh - awsaw. - 'Make', as in create - to originate a species.

As already mentioned, sin, darkness and Satan have colluded to deeply blur this image of God in humankind. When we receive Christ, that image is recaptured. We are born again into the Father's image. We are not just **'created'**. We are **born** of God. We receive the spiritual genetics of the Father when we are born from above. The traits of God manifest in our re-creation. When people meet us they should be feeling like they are experiencing reflections of God in the Earth. We do what God would do; we behave like Jesus Christ would behave. Our character reflects His.

'...the 'image of God' consists in man's mental and moral attributes as a self-conscious, rational, personal agent, capable of self-determination and obedience to moral law. This gives man his position of lordship in creation, and invests his being

with the sanctity of personality.'
(International Standard Bible Encyclopedia)

Calvin stated, *'The image of God is the complete excellence of human nature'.*

The Bible calls us the image and glory of God.

> *1 Corinthians 11:7 For a man indeed ought not to cover his head, since he is the image and glory of God;*

When we live in the 'new man', we live in the image of God. There is a false righteousness and a false holiness. Neither reflects the image of God. The new nature reflects perfectly the true righteousness and the true holiness of the Father.

Through the fall the image of God was seriously attacked, damaged and flawed. It has been the ultimate intention of the Father ever since to restore us to the fullness of His image in this Earth.

> *Romans 8:29 ... predestined TO BE CONFORMED TO THE IMAGE OF HIS SON, that He might be the firstborn among many brethren.*

> *1 Corinthians 15:49 And as we have borne the image of the man of dust, we shall also BEAR THE IMAGE OF THE HEAVENLY MAN.*
> *2 Corinthians 3:18 But we all, with unveiled face, beholding as in a mirror the glory of the Lord, ARE BEING TRANSFORMED INTO THE SAME IMAGE*

from glory to glory, just as by the Spirit of the Lord.

Ephesians 4:24 and that you put on THE NEW MAN WHICH WAS CREATED ACCORDING TO GOD, in true righteousness and holiness.

This image we have been 'made in', is not just a distant reflection of the Almighty. Our intrinsic nature echoes the substance of God Himself. The Scriptures are unbelievably bold.

Psalm 82:6 declares we are 'gods'. Jesus Himself quotes this Scripture in the full sense of what it is saying. When He is accused of blasphemy for claiming to be the Son of God, He draws on this Scripture. In John 10:35 He says that if the Scripture declares we are 'gods'. How then could His opponents possibly have a problem with Him, if He is claiming to merely be the Son of God?

Psalm 8:5 declares we have been made a little lower than 'Elohim'.

Ps 8:5 For You have made him a little lower than the angels, And You have crowned him with glory and honor.

The translators obviously found this too much to interpret as it was, so they made 'Elohim', angels, here and only here. Everywhere else the word is translated God!

WE ARE
A NEW CREATION

2 Corinthians 5:17 Therefore, if anyone is in Christ, he is a new creation; old things have passed away; behold, all things have become new.

Not a renewed person, but a brand new person. AMP - '**A new species of being**'.

So how does God create a new creation?

When the Heavens and Earth were first created they were without form and void...Hebrew - '*tohu bohu*'- *waste and empty, chaotic and confused.*

We have a heaven and earth nature. We are a spiritual person but obviously also an earthly person, both living in the same body. We do what no other creature does. We worship. Animals do not worship, yet the most ancient and untouched peoples in the world do. Making sacrifices through priests, they understand worship. This comes from deep in the spirit of man, something God breathed into us. Something no other creature has. We create music, culture and art. Eternity is in our hearts.

However, just as the Earth was without form and void in the beginning, so we became without form, waste and empty, chaotic and confused until we met Christ. Just as the Holy Spirit hovered over the dark waters covering the Earth, so He moved over our lightless lives. In the beginning of time, when the Word 'Let there be light' came, the Holy Spirit's power blazed through the heavens creating an endless universe. When we receive that same Word of God, our lives are transformed, recreated in the same way.

First, light comes to us, the new creation. This light is life. God divides light from the darkness in us. Now we know the difference. We make the choice to live in the light.

The first man Adam was of the Earth. The second man is from Heaven.

> *1 Corinthians 15:47 The FIRST MAN WAS OF THE EARTH, made of dust; therefore his descendants inherit his dominion in his realm - earth, dust. THE SECOND MAN IS THE LORD FROM HEAVEN. Therefore his descendants rule in his realm - the heavenlies.*
> *48 As was the man of dust, so also are those who are made of dust; and as is the heavenly Man, so also are those who are heavenly.*
> *49 AND AS WE HAVE BORNE THE IMAGE OF THE MAN OF DUST, WE SHALL ALSO BEAR THE IMAGE OF THE HEAVENLY MAN.*

Adam was quite easily deceived. He listened to the temptation, which he knew would lead to disobedience to God. Regardless, he went ahead unmindful of the consequences. Once his 'eyes were opened', he immediately felt something he had not felt before. His innocence was gone. He knew he was naked and he felt shame. Weak and fearful, he and his wife hid from God.

Jesus is truth itself. He is full of light, faith and love. He is filled with the Holy Spirit, anointed, doing good, healing all oppressed by the devil. (Acts 10:38) He is undefeated in temptation, invincible in death, complete master of circumstances.

Our flesh is death dominated. It terminates after 70 or so years. However, our spirit man is invincible. It is '**life-dominated**'.

The natural man is sickness dominated.
The spirit man is health dominated.
The natural man is motivated by flesh.
The spirit man is motivated by Heaven.

Jesus was the exact image of God in the Earth.
Our invisible God purposes to be visible in the Earth.

> *Colossians 1:15 He, Jesus is the image of the invisible God, the firstborn over all creation.*

God entered into His creation. He became incarnate, flesh and blood.

> *1 Timothy 3:16 God was manifested in the flesh, in Christ..*

His image however, was also always to be borne by men and women who also owned their own unique identity. This is one of the most beautiful of all the mysteries of God.

Adam receives dominion over all God has created. As 'Adam' we also receive dominance over all creation.

The new creation man also receives dominion in the invisible, spiritual realm. He reigns over life, death, sickness,

demons, circumstances, sin and self.
Our spirit man is in the image of God.

> *Ephesians 4:24 '...and that you put on the new man which was created according to God...'*

There's not one religious observance, not one religious ceremony, not one religious act you can do, that will bring the salvation of your soul. The only thing that accomplishes the works of God is **being a new creation**.

> *Galatians 6:15 For in Christ Jesus neither circumcision nor uncircumcision AVAILS anything, BUT A NEW CREATION.*

What works in the New Testament is the new creation man. The new nature inherits the New Testament. The old nature would love to have the things the new nature is due to inherit but it is unqualified to obtain those things. The selfishness, doubt, fears and disobedience of the old nature prevent it from receiving the promises.

> *Ezekiel 36:26 I will give you a new heart and put a new spirit within you; I will take the heart of stone out of your flesh and give you a heart of flesh.*

The new man is formed in the image of God. However, this 'new person', new man, new image is not forced upon us. We are in the new man because we **'put on'**, the new man.

Ephesians 4:24 ...PUT ON the new man ... created according to God...

Colossians 3:10 ... have PUT ON the new man...

We step into the new creation person. It's not a feeling thing. We are not grounded on feelings. Our basis for life is the Word of God. We 'put on' dominion. We 'put on' joy. We 'put on' love. We 'put on' forgiveness. We 'put on' health. We 'put on' the new man. The new creation persona doesn't drop on us from the sky. We take the initiative, 'put on' this nature and walk in it, through our decision to do just that! So walk like an overcomer, talk like an overcomer, feel in your heart like an overcomer, be an overcomer!

WE ARE OVERCOMERS

No matter what we face, we are overcomers.

I John 5:4 For whatever is born of God overcomes the world. And this is the victory that has overcome the world - our faith.

When a mother eagle is about to give birth to her young, she scours the countryside for thorny, prickly branches and creates a large bowl on a ledge hundreds of feet up the side of a sheer cliff. Then she gathers softer materials like feathers, wool, cloth and other bedding for the future chicks. After she's settled in she eventually gives birth to her eggs. As time passes each chick breaks out of their egg and mother feeds the ever growing young birds. However, as the birds get older, there comes a day when mother seems to lose her mind. She pulls out all the soft bedding and throws it over the side of their precious ledge. Even though it's uncomfortable the chicks decide to stay in what they know as home. However, mother's insane period has not finished. She now destroys the nest so there's nowhere for the youngsters to stay. Then to their horror mother sweeps them towards the ledge with her great wings. Near the edge she simply sweeps them right off into mid air. The terrified little birds seem to be falling to inevitable death, tumbling through the air. However, then something almost magical happens. The little bird stretches its wings to unexpectedly find itself doing something more exhilarating than it ever believed possible. It discovers it can fly. This would never have happened without something seemingly terrible happening. We don't know what skills we have in Christ until we're in a fight or a storm or troubles, where we need to summon abilities we never knew we had.

We'll never discover we are overcomers until we have something to overcome. Our Christian life moves in the opposite direction to the culture of this age. We find ourselves with far more challenges than we want. Yet, faith to overcome is available whenever we face difficult circumstances, when we fail, when things don't go the way they should. When life is at its worst, we move into faith, the attitude of the overcomer. We declare we're going to make it, that we will win. This won't bury us. We'll only go higher. We accept the fact there will be difficulties, setbacks, but that's OK because we know we'll cross the finish line in victory. We'll beat the odds. Darkness doesn't overpower us. We overcome darkness. That's just how we are. That's how it is. **Defeats don't have to defeat us. Failure doesn't make us a failure.** These things happen. Everybody in life makes a mistake or fails at various times. It's part of living. What we do with those failures, and how we react to those times, is the reason we will either ultimately make it to the other side or not. We overcome.

Glenn Cunningham was given up on by doctors in 1917. They predicted he would spend the rest of his life in a wheelchair, after an explosion burnt his legs at the age of five. 'He'll never walk again,' they said. 'No chance.' His burns were so bad they were going to amputate.

Glenn didn't listen to the doctors. Two years later he started walking again. His mother watched him take hold of an old plow and with a hand on each handle, he made his crippled legs move. Soon he was walking. Then he was jogging; before long he was running. Now he became even more determined.

'I always believed that I could walk, and I did. Now I'm going to run faster than anybody has ever run.' And he did.

Glenn became a great runner who, in 1934, set the world's record for running a mile in 4:06 minutes.

The attitude of an overcomer means that whatever discouraging, seemingly impossible situation we face, we make the effort to overcome. As we do, the power of God will work with that step of faith and we will overcome.

WE ARE SONS OF GOD

When you receive Christ you become a child of God, one of

the sons of God!

As His child you now have an inheritance.

The basis of this New Testament inheritance is Christ in us.

There is nothing we can add to improve that position. We cannot improve our status before God. Christ is far beyond sufficient.

Philippians 3:9 and be found in Him, not having my own righteousness, which is from the law, but that which is through faith in Christ, the righteousness which is from God by faith;

The key to salvation is receiving Christ. The qualification for every spiritual blessing is Christ in us. The basis for salvation or blessing is not our faithfulness as Christians, our maturity, our service to God or our devotional life. All these help appropriate New Testament realities, but understand, it is Christ in us that qualifies us for every promise of God. The fullness of the Godhead resides now in us. Once we have received Christ, His blood washes us completely clean. This makes us fit for God, accepted in the beloved!

> *Colossians 2:9 For in Him dwells all the fullness of the Godhead bodily;*
> *... and you are complete in Him...*

When Christ enters our lives we are born again, from above. Born of God.

The moment we receive Jesus Christ we enter into a contract with God. We will spend time and eternity unraveling all Jesus has accomplished for us.

Psalm 92:4 For You, LORD, have made me glad through Your work; I will triumph in the works of Your hands.

We 'have been' blessed. We are not trying to get blessed. We are, right now, already blessed. There is nothing we can do to improve on Christ in us. We can offer nothing that would add value to Christ. No, our journey is **unpackaging this gift.** We pray. We feed on His Word. We awaken to what has been achieved for us. We appropriate it. We make it real.

When Jesus died upon the cross, His last words were, **'It is finished'.**

He had accomplished a **complete salvation.**

From here He simply trusted Himself to the Father. **'Into your hands I commit my spirit' Luke 23:46...** the greatest act of faith, ever. There's nothing you can do when you're dead. No amount of 'positive mental attitude' will get you up again. No matter how motivated you are before you die, when you're dead, you're dead. Another power beyond your own has to come into play. Jesus connected with that resurrection power through faith. God raised Him from the dead.

This same God had told Joshua He **has** given him the entire land of Canaan. (Joshua 1:3). The truth is, it has actually been theirs for forty years. Tragically, because they had refused to believe God, they had not been able to 'unpackage' this gift. However, now a leader and a generation who believe God get together, and they are able to begin possessing their possessions.

Obadiah 1:17 'But on Mount Zion...the house of Jacob

shall possess their possessions.

It seems a highly unusual statement that the house of Jacob would possess their possessions. If we possess something, why is there any need to still possess it? This is the constant truth of New Testament life. Even though we may possess the same inheritance as Jesus Christ, it remains dormant unless we constantly step into possessing that inheritance. We must choose to walk by faith in the Word.

Paul immediately makes the connection between sonship and inheritance. Almost every time he mentions sonship he goes straight to inheritance. This was a strong association in the mind of any Hebrew. However, Paul's use of the term is also in the light of the Romans understanding of inheritance. Contrary to the well-known maxim of English law, *Nemo est heres viventis* 'No one is heir of the living', according to Roman law, the moment a child was born he was his father's heir.

> *Galatians 3:26 For you are all sons of God through faith in Christ Jesus.*

We have an inheritance, not because we are keepers of a law, but because we have received Christ into our lives. Because of **Him and Him alone, we have an inheritance.**

> *Romans 8:17   and if children, then heirs - heirs of God and joint heirs with Christ, if indeed we suffer with Him, that we may also be glorified together.*

WE ARE
KINGS, RULING IN OUR WORLD.

Revelation 1:6 ... has made us kings and priests to His God and Father...'

The apostle Peter also declares;

1 Peter 2:9 But you are a chosen generation, a ROYAL PRIESTHOOD, a holy nation, His own special people, that you may proclaim the praises of Him who called you out of darkness into His marvelous light;

As soon as we receive Christ we are born into royalty. As He is a King so are we. We are born into kingship. **We are born to rule and to reign with Him.**

Romans 5:17 TLB - The sin of this one man, Adam, caused death to be king over all, but all who will take God's gift of forgiveness and acquittal are KINGS OF LIFE because of this one man, Jesus Christ.

When the disciples are sinking in their boat because of an enormous storm, they run to Jesus to help them, however, there's a problem, He's asleep. Theirs is the deepest felt distress they've ever known, yet their Saviour is calmly asleep! How could this be when they're in such danger? They immediately accuse Him of being uncaring. 'Do you not care that we are perishing?' (Mark 4:38) When we interpret God's attitude towards us through our circumstances, we will always arrive at wrong conclusions. His heart towards us is revealed through the Word of God. This is the only and final authority in every circumstance for the believer to live by. When we fail to rise up in faith, we will arise with accusations against God for not doing what we expected He would. However, He is wanting **us** to do those things that we are waiting for Him to do.

God sleeps so WE will wake up.

Awake to what? To who we are and what we have. We have lived under 'wilderness conditions' for too long. 'Wilderness conditions' is where we expect God to do it all, to make water pour from a rock, provide bread and meat from heaven, cover us from heat in the day with a cloud, and warm us with a pillar of fire at night. However, God is unwilling for us to stay in this position - where He does it all. He intends that we'll begin to rule in life taking charge over our circumstances. We're the ones meant to be slaying the giants. Not God! He'll help. He'll move in our moving. But He's trying to get you and I to discover the power He's deposited in us. Sometimes God seems asleep, completely ignoring our prayers. Why? He's drawing up from within us our birthright, to be ruling in life, kings in the Earth. The degree of our authority reflects the degree of our submission. We have submitted ourselves to Christ, the Ruler of the Universe. We've submitted ourselves to the will of God by receiving His Son as our Saviour and Lord. Our purpose now is to implement the will of God through the authority He has deposited within us. Any crisis we face is designed to help us discover that power within us.

WE ARE
THE GLORY OF THE LORD

2 Corinthians 3:18 But we all, with unveiled face, beholding as in a mirror the glory of the Lord, are being transformed into the same image from glory to glory, just as by the Spirit of the Lord.

The Word says we are the 'glory of God'. The Word is a mirror. We look into this mirror. The reflected image is the glory of God. This transforms us. The Spirit transforms us. We see ourselves like He sees us. We transform into that same image. We transform into the glory of the Lord.

The word 'glory' means to 'to make magnificent and have a good opinion of'. Jesus said He gives us the same glory the Father had given Him!

John 17:22 And the glory which You gave Me I have given them,

Jesus did not come to shame us, upbraid us, reproach us, but to 'glorify' us. 'them He also glorified'(Romans 8:30)

What God the Father said to His Son Jesus, He also says to us. The same glory He gave to Jesus, Jesus gives to us! Not only does the Lord remove guilt and shame from us, but He also now showers us with His glory. This manifests in our lives in honor, ennoblement and blessing. God is glorified by us, His children also being honored in life. There is no honor to a father when his children live in shame, dishonor and reproach. All our reproaches have fallen upon Jesus, so the same glory may also fall upon us. God has planned a life of glory for each of His children. No matter what our circumstances are as we accept that God in Heaven has honored us, we will have a posture within that will eventually be reflected in our circumstances without.

We look into our future and we see the glory of God. When you imagine yourself in years to come, see yourself blessed in every way. The greatest blessing is to be on the journey of being changed into the glory of the Lord. This has always been the Father's ultimate intention for all of us.

> *NKJV says - Jeremiah 29:11 For I know the thoughts that I think toward you, says the LORD, thoughts of peace and not of evil, to give you a future and a hope.*

> *RSV says - Jeremiah 29:11... plans for welfare and not for evil...*

> *NAS says - Jeremiah 29:11 ...plans for welfare and not for calamity ...*

> *NIV says - Jeremiah 29:11 ...plans to prosper you and not to harm you...*

All the plans of God for us are for good, not disaster. He determines to manifest His glory in our future.

The opposite to glory is shame. He hasn't called you to shame, He's called you to glory.

> *Rom 8:30 '...these He also glorified.*

God considers you the saints, the magnificent ones!

Paul writes his letter to those who are **'saints in Christ Jesus.'**
(Ephesians 1:1)

This is the basis for all of Paul's thinking, emphasized more than any of the other New Testament writers, that we become elevated in everything in life by being in Christ.

In most people's minds the word 'saints' has come to mean only a select few people, now passed on, but who lived exceptionally ascetic lives or who have had miracles attributed to them.

Here's the criteria the Catholic church holds to, for the canonization of these past members.

Two verifiable postmortem miracles
Note: Canonization sainthood requires two miracles, whereas beatification, blessed requires only one.

Evidence of having led an exemplary life of goodness and virtue worthy of imitation, having died a heroic death of martyrdom, or having undergone a major conversion of heart where a previous immoral life is abandoned and replaced by one of outstanding holiness. Formally declared saints are chosen ultimately by the Pope, but only after a thorough investigation of the life, writings, and legacy of the saint candidate. No stone is left unturned. Testimony from witnesses and experts, physical evidence, and the entire life of the person is examined with fine detail.

However, Paul is not writing to dead people, or those who have performed miracles, or who have even lived exemplary lives. He recognizes they are saints simply because they are 'in Christ'.

We become who we believe we are. Part of the role of a minister is to reveal to people who they actually are, so they can walk the pathway towards being exactly that.

Saints are people who are complete, perfect and undefiled by this world, qualified for Heaven by the grace of God, which has imparted the life of Christ to each believer, freely. Saints are the magnificent ones of God. If we are to think of ourselves as the magnificent ones, how would we live differently?

You have been made holy and beyond reproach, beyond condemnation, beyond shame, in Christ.

> *Col 1:21, 22 'And you, who once were alienated and enemies in your mind by wicked works, yet now He has reconciled...*
> *in the body of His flesh through death, to present you holy, and blameless, and above reproach in His sight.'*

WE ARE
MORE THAN CONQUERORS

> *Romans 8:37 Yet in all these things we are more than conquerors through Him who loved us.*

We are 'more than conquerors' because all the conquering that can be done has been done... by Jesus!

As He died on the cross, He cried out, 'It is finished'. He had accomplished the full salvation of man through the work of the cross. Being more than a conqueror means there is nothing more to conquer. The devil is conquered, sin is conquered along with sickness, death, hell, self, poverty, and the curse. All has been conquered on our behalf. Now we are seated with Christ, reigning with Him in this life.

Paul has just completed listing all the trials, tribulations, persecutions and trouble he and his team had been through, but then declares that in all these things they experienced the overcoming, conquering power of God.

We live near the beach and when tourists who are unfamiliar with the surf swim in the ocean, they often find the waves overwhelming. They struggle to stay on their feet and keep their head above the water. Yet, a little further out there are surfers riding those very same waves that threaten to drown others. In a way those surfers have become more than conquerors. They're not just not drowning under the waves; they're totally loving the thrill of riding them. There are any number of troubling situations that threaten to drown people in our world, but we, the believers, should be able to live above these with a victory and a joy that can only come from overcoming through Christ.

WHAT DO
WE HAVE

1. WE HAVE DOMINION AND AUTHORITY

Romans 5:17 For if by the one man's offense death reigned through the one, much more those who receive abundance of grace and of the gift of righteousness will REIGN IN LIFE through the One, Jesus Christ.

Instead of death reigning, now we reign in life.
Health reigns, instead of sickness.
Life reigns instead of death.
Light reigns instead of darkness.
Wealth reigns instead of poverty.
Solutions reign instead of problems.

Death, like a monarch, sat enthroned on the sin of Adam. But Jesus defeated death through living a righteous life and dying a sacrificial death. Jesus destroyed sin and the dominion it had held since the garden of Eden. Now death has no throne, no power. Death has no rule over anyone with Christ in their life. If we rule over the final enemy - death, then everything else is also under our dominion.

Speaking of you and I, David says;

> *Ps 8:6 You have made him man to have dominion over the works of Your hands; you have put all things under his feet.*

This says God has granted us complete authority to reign in this life. The way this has occurred is through freely receiving the gift of the righteousness of Christ. Our original representative man, Adam, succumbed to the devil, thereby giving him authority over his life, also inadvertently bringing all his subsequent offspring, (the entire human race., under the dominion of the devil. The second representative man, Jesus Christ, obeyed God rather than submitting to the devil, and therefore gained back all authority, not only in Earth, but also in Heaven. This is passed on to all His subsequent 'offspring', those who are born again by receiving Christ.

> *Rom 5:17 For if by the one man's offense death reigned through the one, much more those who receive abundance of grace and of the gift of righteousness will reign in life through the One, Jesus Christ.*

The Jamieson, Fausset, and Brown Commentary says, *'the whole statement amounts to this: 'If one man's one offence let loose against us the tyrant power of Death, to hold us as its victims in helpless bondage, 'much more,' when we stand forth enriched with God's abounding grace,' and in the beauty of a complete absolution from countless offences, shall we expatiate in a life divinely owned and legally secured, 'reigning' in exultant freedom and unchallenged might.*

Adam was the head of the old creation. Christ is the Head of the new creation. Jesus is the Last Adam (1 Corinthians. 15:45-49) The OT is the 'book of the generations of Adam' (Genesis. 5:1) It ends speaking of a curse (Malachi. 4:6) The NT is the 'book of the generation of Jesus Christ' (Matthew. 1:1) It ends with 'no more curse'.
(Revelation 22:3)

Jesus reigned, reigns and will reign forever in this life and every other life. He has conquered death itself. Nothing else remains to be defeated and subjugated to Christ. He rules! I'm on His side. I'm inextricably linked to Him, united with Him, sharing His victory and power. My purpose in life is to now subjugate those areas not yet under His dominion. **We are implementing and appropriating** the victory Christ has won. Where sickness still exists in this world it is only because we have not implemented the healing of Christ through the cross. Where devils still oppress people it is because we have not yet taken dominion over them. Poverty rules in people's lives because we have not brought the prosperity of Christ.

Because He reigns, I reign.
He rules, I rule.
I'm in Him. He's in me.
He rules over sickness and disease.
I rule over sickness and disease.
He rules over devils. I rule over devils.
I act in His Name.
His power is the same as it ever was.

Instead of death reigning, we now reign in life.
We are health, instead of sickness, we are life instead of death, we are light instead of darkness, we are wealth instead of poverty, and we have solutions for the problems people face.

There is not a problem God has not already provided the answer for.

There is not a problem any of us face that is bigger than the God inside us.

There is not a problem mankind faces that cannot be solved

through the complete salvation of the cross of Christ.

Again let me say, even though death has sat like a monarch enthroned on the sin of Adam, Jesus has defeated death through a righteous life. Now death has no throne, no power. Death cannot rule over a person with Christ in their life. Sin cannot rule over a person with Christ in their life. Sickness cannot rule over people with Christ in their lives. This is truth waiting to be appropriated. Believe the Word of God. Stand in your position. Hold your ground in the work of the cross.

> *1 Corinthians 15:25 For He must reign till He has put all enemies under His feet.*
> *... For 'HE HAS PUT ALL THINGS UNDER HIS FEET.'*

The Pulpit Commentary London; New York: Funk & Wagnalls Company cites H. D. M. Spence-Jones, Ed, *1 Corinthians*. 1909;

"Last of enemies doomed to annulment is Death;" or, as in Tyndale's version. "Lastly, Death the enemy shall be destroyed;" or, as in the Rhemish Version, "And at the last, Death the enemy shall be destroyed." The present, "is being annulled," is the *præsens futurascens*, or the present of which the accomplishment is regarded as already begun and continuing by an inevitable law. Death and Hades and the devil, "who hath the power of death," are all doomed to abolition.

So, even though at present it seems as though not everything is actually under the feet of Christ, we are on that journey of implementing the ultimate victory of Christ on the Cross, until the end of this age, when all his enemies will be finally vanquished.

> *1 Peter 3:22 Christ who has gone into heaven and is at the right hand of God, angels and authorities and powers HAVING BEEN MADE SUBJECT TO HIM.*

Dominion in life is a believer's privilege. God has given us dominion in this life to implement His finished victories.

Are we at the mercy of whatever life brings us?
Do we have any control over what happens to us in our lives?
Do we have control over our circumstances?

God has given the believer dominion over sin, the devil, sickness and circumstances.

The moment we are born again we receive authority, the same authority that a son or daughter of a King have in their father's Kingdom.

> *John 1:12 But as many as received Him, to them He gave the right to become children of God, to those who believe in His name:*

The word '**right**' (Greek - 'exousia'), literally means -

> *power of choice, liberty of doing as one pleases, permission physical and mental power, the ability or strength with which one is endued, which he either possesses or exercises the power of authority (influence) and of right (privilege)*

the power of rule or government (the power of him whose will and commands must be submitted to by others and obeyed)
universally, authority over mankind

the power of judicial decisions
of authority to manage domestic affairs
a thing subject to authority or rule, jurisdiction, one who possesses authority, a ruler, a human magistrate
the leading and more powerful among created beings superior to man, spiritual potentates
the sign of regal authority, a crown

Our dominion is based in these two facts;
- God has all authority.
- He has given that authority to us.

A police officer wears a uniform to identify his authority. Other people in positions of power use their signature. For some, a simple nod indicates their authority. For us, we exercise our authority through the name of Jesus.

When we obey God, we are acting in His Name. When we act in His character, we are acting in His Name. He has given us His Name so we have the authority to achieve those things that align with the will and character of God. He has always revealed Himself through His Name. He is known through His Name. His character is understood through His Name. If we do something 'in the Name of' God, then we reveal a characteristic of that name. His purposes are revealed in His Name. To act in His Name is to fulfill a purpose of God. All the Names of God throughout the Old Testament are now fulfilled in just one Name, that is, the Name of Jesus. God has invested the entire authority of Heaven into this Name. He has given that Name to every believer to use. When we act in that name, we let loose the power of Christ to do His will in the Earth.

KEY ELEMENTS TO OUR AUTHORITY

——— THE NAME OF JESUS CHRIST ———

We are authorized to act in His Name on His behalf as the power of attorney for the God of Heaven on Earth. At law the person with power of attorney is able to conduct transactions on behalf of another person who has given them their authority to do so. Jesus has given us His authority by giving us His Name. When we have Christ in us, we also have His Name. If God Himself were to visit the Earth and command certain things to happen you and I both know, there would not be anything that could resist that command. His Word would happen. Jesus was God in the flesh on earth, commanding sickness to leave, demons to be cast out, the dead to be raised and all manner of other supernatural things. No situation remained the same after He had spoken the Word to it. Well, that same authority has now been given to you and me. That's the power of His Name. He has given us His authority by giving us His Name. When we have Christ in us, we have His Name upon us.

If you go out on the highway and attempt to stop a road train by jutting your shoulder up against the grill, you won't win. You'll be a spot on the road. However, if you put on a policeman's uniform, stand in the middle of the road and simply raise your hand, amazingly the truck will brake to a halt. The uniform indicates that you have authority. The might of the entire government is backing you up. This is exactly the same with what you have in Christ. We are clothed with Christ and the power of the Holy Spirit. We have authority. We have the power of attorney. We can speak and act in the Name of Jesus and expect that God's power will manifest.

> *Mark 16:17 IN MY NAME they will cast out demons.*

> *John 14:13 Whatever you ask IN MY NAME, that I will do.*

> *John 14:14 If you ask anything IN MY NAME, I will do it.*

> *John 16:23 Whatever you ask the father IN MY NAME He will give you.*

The Name of Jesus carries incredible power in Earth.

Acts 19 records the story where some exorcists try to use the Name of Jesus, but fail. The demons did not submit to the authority of the exorcists because they were not operating in the power of Christ. The Name of Jesus is not some magical incantation. Using the Name of Jesus is acting on behalf of Jesus, acting for His glory not ours, acting in His interests, not ours. We can only do this when He is centrally located in our hearts. Both Heaven and Hell recognize when Christ dwells within a person and they in Him.

In stark contrast, Acts 3 recounts the story of Peter and John releasing the power God through the Name of Jesus as they heal the man with disabled legs at the Gate Beautiful. Peter sees the man begging for money. He tells him he doesn't have anything to give him except the healing power of God. Peter commands the man to stand and walk, in the Name of Jesus. The man who had never walked in his entire life, walks, because someone invoked healing upon him through the name of Jesus Christ.

OBEDIENCE

Our authority comes from our submission to the will of God. This will is revealed both generally and specifically.

We obey and therefore rule.
We are both servant and master.
We both obey and command.
The extent of the authority over us is the extent of the authority we command.

> *Matthew 8:5 Now when Jesus had entered Capernaum, a centurion came to Him, pleading with Him,*
> *6 saying, 'Lord, my servant is lying at home paralyzed, dreadfully tormented.'*
> *7 And Jesus said to him, 'I will come and heal him.'*
> *8 The centurion answered and said, 'Lord, I am not worthy that You should come under my roof. But only speak a word, and my servant will be healed.*
> *9 'For I also am a man under authority, having soldiers*

under me. And I say to this one, 'Go,' and he goes; and to another, 'Come,' and he comes; and to my servant, 'Do this,' and he does it.'

10 When Jesus heard it, He marveled, and said to those who followed, 'Assuredly, I say to you, I have not found such great faith, not even in Israel!

11 'And I say to you that many will come from east and west, and sit down with Abraham, Isaac, and Jacob in the kingdom of heaven.

12 'But the sons of the kingdom will be cast out into outer darkness. There will be weeping and gnashing of teeth.'

13 Then Jesus said to the centurion, 'Go your way; and as you have believed, so let it be done for you.' And his servant was healed that same hour.

This soldier understood authority. He lived or died by it. He understood that if he commanded a soldier to do something, the soldier would obey, because all the might of Rome backed the command. The soldier had no choice. Jesus had authority over *'the soldiers'* of healing. The Centurion knew that he did not have authority in this area of healing, but that Jesus did. Jesus was not here to command Roman soldiers. He was not a representative of Rome's authority, but He was a representative of God's authority and so He was well able to exercise that authority in the Earth. He ruled over sickness. He ruled over death. He lived as the Son of God whilst here on Earth. He executed authority as the Son of God.

The soldier also understood he only needed to speak to exercise authority. He didn't have to go to the soldier he was commanding. He simply had to send a command.

The authority of Jesus is exercised exactly the same way, through speaking commands. When we believe in the words of our mouth carrying the authority of Heaven, we are able to speak to circumstance and see them transformed.

Jesus also declared that we can rule over natural elements in this world simply through the words of our mouth.

> *Luke 8:25 But He said to them, 'Where is your faith?' And they were afraid, and marveled, saying to one another, 'Who can this be? For He commands even the winds and water, and they obey Him!'*

When He asks them, 'Where is your faith?' He is referring to the fact that they could have done exactly the same as what He did, if they had just commanded the storm to stop, believing that what they said would happen.

> *Matthew 28:18-19 And Jesus came and spoke to them, saying, 'All authority has been given to Me in heaven and on earth. Go therefore and make disciples of all the nations.'*

Jesus has given us the right to use His authority.
What authority did (does) Jesus have? All!
What did (does) he have authority over? Everything!

We have all authority over every obstacle against the Gospel reaching the world. Same with the building of the Church and the making of disciples.

Matthew 7:28-29 When Jesus had finished saying these things, the crowds were amazed at his teaching, because he taught as one who had authority, and not as their teachers of the law.

Apparently the 'man on the street' had heard the local preachers many times. Now however, in comparison with Jesus, the most striking difference was his authority. Jesus spoke without any doubtfulness, without pleading, but with bold, confident, faith filled declarations - authority. There are many teachers, because gathering information and then repeating that data is not hard. However, to emerge from the Presence of God with an assignment from heaven calls for a price to be paid. Jesus was that man. He spoke as a man with a mandate, a prophet with a Word!

When we speak, Peter tells us to speak as the oracles of God (1 Peter 4:11). Our vocal posture determines our level of spiritual impartation. Demons flee, miracles happen and people respond to God because we speak boldly, with authority, the same authority That Jesus Himself had on Earth.

THE PROMISES OF GOD

2 Peter 1:3... as His divine power has given to us all things that pertain to life and godliness, through the knowledge of Him who called us by glory and virtue, by which have been given to us exceedingly great and precious promises, that through these you may be partakers of the divine nature, having escaped the corruption that is in the world through lust.

There is one thing God cannot do...lie!

The Scripture cannot be broken. Once God has uttered a statement it is impossible for it to not come to pass. The entire Universe is held together by the veracity of God's Word. His Word will not fail. We can stake our lives on His promises. Our authority is in His promises. Over the years of being a pastor when people in our church have faced serious illnesses, I have given them a list of promises to speak and meditate on. This has proved to release incredible power as they speak the Word of God. The power of the Holy Spirit accompanies the Word and His power brings healing.

The promises of God become the power of God when they are believed and acted upon.

THE PRINCIPLES OF GOD

No matter who we are, young, old, male, female, short, tall, rich or poor - the principles of God in creation will work for us when we simply activate them. Anyone can cause a plant to grow by planting a seed and watering it. Sowing seed is a principle of God in the natural world as well as in the spiritual. Giving a gift is described as an act of sowing according to Scripture. When we give, we exercise a principle of God. The forces of nature work together to cause a seed to sprout from the ground. In the same way, the principles of God work to bring back into people's lives what they have given to others and to God.

Psalm 8:6 You have made him to have dominion over the works of Your hands; you have put all things under his feet.

We exercise that dominion over the Earth by employing the principles of God.

—— WE HAVE AUTHORITY OVER THE DEVIL ——

Phil 2:10 that at the name of Jesus every knee should bow, of those in heaven, and of those on earth, and of those under the earth.

Jesus has imparted the same authority He had over demons, to us. His perfect life has given the devil zero legal rights to any area of His life. He has imputed that perfect life to anyone who receives Him. He defeated the devil in hell and took from him the keys of hell and death, so the devil no longer has this power. Jesus has given this to us, so that we can rule over death and hell.

Luke 10:19 Behold, I give you the authority to trample on serpents and scorpions, and over all the power of the enemy, and nothing shall by any means hurt you.

Matthew 10:1 He called his twelve disciples to him and gave them authority to drive out evil spirits and to heal every disease and sickness.

In both these Scriptures, we are told Jesus gave authority to His disciples. How did He give it to them? He spoke it. We exercise authority and we give authority by speaking it into people's lives.

He may also have laid hands on them. This is what Paul reminded Timothy of when he told him to stir up the gift which he had received through laying on of hands and prophecy (1 Timothy 4:14). Throughout the Book of Acts time and again, people afflicted with demons were set free through the power of the Name of Jesus.

> *Mark 16:17 And these signs will accompany those who believe: In my name they will drive out demons; they will speak in new tongues.*

> *Acts 5:16 Crowds gathered also from the towns around Jerusalem, bringing their sick and those tormented by evil spirits, and all of them were healed.*

> *Acts 8:7 With shrieks, evil spirits came out of many, and many paralytics and cripples were healed.*

> *Acts 19:12 so that even handkerchiefs and aprons that had touched him were taken to the sick, and their illnesses were cured and the evil spirits left them.*

2. WE HAVE THE WISDOM OF GOD

How wise do we imagine God is? This would be impossible, way beyond our perceptions. All the wisdom there is comes from God Himself. The wisdom to engineer a never ending universe, employing forces like gravity to suspend utterly enormous planets and suns in space. The wisdom that designs a thousand systems within the Earth, and in the human body to bring health, reproduction, food, water, air, and everything else needed to sustain life. The wisdom of God seen in all creation, spiritual and natural to bring about both beautiful and useful plants, animals, music, scenes, and the crowning glory of man behaving in his highest attributes, bringing goodness and love in families and friends. This same wisdom has become ours in Christ.

> *1 Corinthians 1:30 You are in Christ Jesus, who became for us wisdom from God.*

> *1 Corinthians 2:16 But we have the mind of Christ.*

I've looked through many commentaries and translations on this verse. It's almost impossible to find one that agrees with this Scripture, that is, that we actually do have the mind of Christ. This is because people walk by their natural senses. If we can't feel a thing then we simply can't believe it's true. However, just because we can't see it, touch it, taste it or feel it, doesn't mean it's not true. This is what walking by faith is all about. If the Bible says we have the mind of Christ then that is what we have, whether we 'experience' it or not. Believing the Word and acting on it makes it become reality. The Bible is truth waiting to be manifested. In fact we are told the entire creation groans for the manifestation of the sons of God (Romans 8:20). The bridge between truth on pages and reality in circumstances is simply faith in action.

3. WE HAVE POWER FROM THE SPIRIT

Micah 3:8 But truly I am full of power by the Spirit of the LORD,

Luke 24:49 Behold, I send the Promise of My Father upon you; but tarry in the city of Jerusalem until you are endued with power from on high.

When the Holy Spirit becomes part of our lives we are filled with the same power that created the entire universe. Jesus knew the job He had given us was beyond our own strength and so He commanded the disciples to make sure they received power from on high before they attempted to fulfill His plan. After ten days of waiting in the Upper Room, they were baptised in the power of the Holy Spirit on the Day of Pentecost. (Acts 2) From that point those early disciples were completely transformed men and women. The most dramatic turnaround was Peter, who just days before was a discouraged, dejected fisherman who felt he had completely failed Christ, having denied him three times. Yet, after being baptised in the Holy Spirit he fearlessly stands before a crowd of devoted religious people proclaiming Christ, bringing three thousand of them to Christ in a moment! All the disciples literally turned the world upside down with their preaching, miracles and healings after they had been baptised in the power of the Spirit. This power is the same that Samson used to defeat hundreds of warriors single handedly. This is the same power that healed the sick through Jesus. This is the same power that raised Jesus Christ from the dead after three days. This exact same power dwells inside each of us. We can never again admit to being powerless in the face of trouble. Jesus promised the power of the Spirit to all those that hunger for Him. God will satisfy our hunger for Him with the infilling of the Holy Spirit.

4. WE HAVE FREEDOM FROM THE DEVIL

I John 5:18 We know that whoever is born of God does not sin; but he who has been born of God keeps himself, and the wicked one does not touch him.

In Christ we have become a devil free zone. We have complete authority over the devil, just like you have authority over your dog. You tell it to go outside the house, it goes, (well, maybe, but it should!) Just like you have authority over your kids. You tell them to go to bed. They go. (Again!!?) If they don't, you get some more authority in your voice. You know you're the one in control. You take control and the dog goes outside, the kids go to bed. Similarly we have been given complete authority over the devil. All we need to do is exercise it.

THE LIBERATING POWER OF TRUTH

John 8:31 Then Jesus said to those Jews who believed Him, 'If you abide in My word, you are My disciples indeed. 'And you shall know the truth, and the truth shall make you free.'(...and the truth will become a liberating force within you...)

All of us at some stage of life need to be set free from something. This may be an addiction, a habit, depression, emotional wounds, physical disease or anything that has bound us up. We can be set free when someone prays for us. Sometimes a supernatural encounter with the power of God sets us free. These things do happen at times. They are powerful moments. But nothing is as powerful as the liberating force of the Word of God. The most enduring, life transforming, eternity building freedom you can assimilate into your life is from the impact of the Word of God traveling deep into your psyche, into your sub consciousness, into your emotional architecture, into your character, into the essence of who you are.

Religious traditions can't, won't and don't transform us. In fact Jesus said we make the Word of God of no effect through the traditions of man.

> *Mark 7:13 …making the word of God of no effect through your tradition which you have handed down.*

Freedom comes when the Word takes root deep in our soul and goes to work forming the character of God within us.

Isaiah declared that the ways of God are vastly different to the ways of man;

> *Isaiah 55:9 For as the heavens are higher than the earth, so are My ways higher than your ways, and My thoughts than your thoughts.*

We can become convinced of things that appear good yet their end is disastrous. Even though a concept may seem logical, and therefore seem reasonable to believe, if it does not align with the Word of God then we should not receive it.

Proverbs 14:12 There is a way that seems right to a man, but its end is the way of death.

The truth of the Word is vastly different to the truth of man. The natural man invents religious 'truths' that appear good, but are actually not truth at all. At best they are just good concepts, and at worst are the teaching of demons.

Paul told Timothy that the Holy Spirit had revealed to him that the teaching from demons would infiltrate the church. These teachings included forbidding people to marry and commanding them to abstain from eating certain foods.

1Timothy 4:1
Now the Spirit expressly says that in latter times some will depart from the faith, giving heed to deceiving spirits and doctrines of demons.

This abstinence can appear like a godly thing. It appears these religious people have given up such a lot. We become intimidated, thinking they are so holy, yet the Bible says that when a group requires abstinence from marriage, it is the teaching of demons. Part of the harvest of this teaching is the sexual abuse of children and homosexuality. These people are physically frustrated because of a restraint imposed, not by God, but by the teachings of devils! Sexuality within marriage is a beautiful and normal human gift God has endowed us with. When people have unclean minds they cannot conceive of any sex as being holy, let alone, from God! Yet God created us, as we are, with all the parts of our bodies that deliver pleasure. He gave us sex to be enjoyed, but He placed strong limitations around this powerful drive. When people are not gifted by God to a life of celibacy, (and only a very few are), and if religion bans what is right and permissible, then those people will, in frustration, break out in some other area. We most often think that the devil is only involved in tempting people to immoral sins, however, he is just as involved in luring people, through their sincerity into religious bondage. These teachings gain access through people holding to their natural, sincere thinking rather than the Word of God.

Abiding in the Word is having a mind that dwells on Scripture throughout all our days. It is the centrepiece of our thoughts. It is our delight in conversations. It brings a smile to our lips as we meditate in our heart on its precepts.

> *Psalm 1:2 But his delight is in the law of the LORD, and in His law he meditates day and night.*

> *Joshua 1:8 This Book of the Law shall not depart from your mouth, but you shall meditate in it day and night, that you may observe to do according to all that is written in it. For then you will make your way prosperous, and then you will have good success.*

Even though Joshua was a mighty general and warrior; even though he was one of only two spies who brought back a positive report about Canaan and therefore survived the forty years in the wilderness, it was his love for the Word that would be the secret for making his ways successful.

Psalm 119:97 Oh, how I love Your law! It is my meditation all the day.

Abiding in the Word is meditating on the Bible and speaking the Scriptures to ourselves and others.

Abiding in the Word is loving the Word. It is being emotionally attached to the Word.

When the Bible becomes what we think about, rather than the latest movies, magazines, books, TV shows, then we will experience its transforming power. If we eat bad food we get sick and may even die. When we 'eat' unhealthy, unclean words our spirit gets sick. We become dead in our spirit because of the words of death we have permitted to have access to our mind. Conversely the Word of God brings 'life' to our inner man.

Job 23:12 I have treasured the words of His mouth more than my necessary food.

Psalms 40:8 Your law is within my heart.

Psalms 119:72 The law of Your mouth is better to me than thousands of coins of gold and silver.

Jeremiah 15:16 Your words were found, and I ate them, and Your word was to me the joy and rejoicing of my heart.

Abiding in the Word is searching the Word for wisdom, direction, comfort and instruction.
Living in the Word is digesting the life of the Word in our inner man.

Matthew 4:4 But He answered and said, 'It is written, Man shall not live by bread alone, but by every word that proceeds from the mouth of God.'

James 1:21 Therefore lay aside all filthiness and overflow of wickedness, and receive with meekness the implanted word, which is able to save your souls.

The Amplified Bible expands the word 'save' to 'contains the power to save your souls.' So, just like a seed, the Word implanted within the soil of our hearts, grows into a Christ-like nature woven through our own personality.

The Word is a river of truth flowing from the throne.
The Word brings us into our inheritance and our inheritance into us.

Acts 20:32 I commend you to God and to the word of His grace, which is able to build you up and give you an inheritance among all those who are sanctified.

5. WE HAVE GOD FOR US

Romans 8:31 What then shall we say to these things? If God is for us, who can be against us?

This could read… Because God is on our side no-one can oppose us successfully.

King Jehoshaphat in 2 Chronicles 20, discovered that God was for him when he defeated an army vastly outnumbering his own. God told him to simply send worshippers to the front to sing. The enemy army was a confederacy of three nations. As the Israelites went into battle worshipping the Lord, the enemy became divided. They imagined each was attacking the other. This is how they were defeated. They destroyed each other! Jehoshaphat and his army didn't have to do anything at all, except to worship. God is for us. If we will commit our way to Him, listen to His guidance and follow it, we will enjoy the many victories he has already planned for us.

Joshua found that God was for him when he faced enormous giant warriors in the land of Canaan. Time and again the inexperienced Israelites completely defeated the Canaanites as they simply did what the Lord told them to do.

David found that God was for him when he rescued a lamb from his flock out of the mouth of a lion. He found God was for him when he did the same with a bear. He found God was for him when he ran to the giant Goliath -flinging a stone at the great hulk of a man, which brought the Philistine to the ground.

Three boys in Daniel 3:12 found God was for them when they refused to worship any other than Jehovah. The furious king threw them into the fiery furnace. They walked about in the fire unburnt. A fourth man walked among them. It was

Jesus. He was with them and for them.

Moses found God was with him when he single-handedly delivered three million Hebrews from Egypt.

Daniel found God was with him when he was thrown into a den full of ravenous lions, yet they didn't eat him.

Gideon found God was for him when he warred against the mighty Midianite army and defeated them, even though his own army had been reduced to just three hundred men.

Paul found God was for him all his life while he was repeatedly attacked, whipped, stoned, persecuted, yet no-one was able to stop him until his time to die as a martyr came in Rome.

Once we have received Christ, we are in Him, and He in us. This is the New Covenant. In this state, part of the covenant is that God is for us, not based on whether we deserve it or not, but by the grace of God Himself. He has committed Himself to any and everyone who receives His Son and embraces the New Covenant. It is automatic. If you have Christ, then God is for you!

Let me repeat this mighty Scripture;

> *Romans 8:31 What then shall we say to these things? If God is for us, who can be against us?*

The next verse carries just as much weight;

Romans 8:32 He who did not spare His own Son, but delivered Him up for us all, how shall He not with Him also freely give us all things?

This is easily one of the most powerful arguments of Scripture. (This also reminds us of that moment when Abraham did not hold back his only son also, showing God there was nothing he would hold back from Jehovah.) In the reverse of that thought we can understand that, if God will not withhold His only Son from us, then there is nothing else in Earth or in the Universe that He will or could withhold. To withhold anything else would be to say it had more value than His own Son. (JFB -- *all other gifts being not only immeasurably less than this gift of gifts, but virtually included in it.*)

Anything God gives us will never be worth more than Christ. We all have needs and desires. Is Christ worth more than the things we desire or need? Obviously! He is all I need. So God is delighted to fulfill our prayers and grant us the desires of our hearts. He will do this in His timing, His way. He supplies our needs and fulfills our dreams.

Virtually every page of Scripture recounts stories of God providing people's needs. The Israelites received bread from heaven in the wilderness. Out of a rock poured water enough for three million people. Elijah camped by the brook Cherith and had food brought to him daily by ravens during a famine in Israel. Then when the brook dried up, God led him to a widow in Zarephath. This woman received the extraordinary miracle that her flour bin would never empty no matter how much she used. When the people listening to Jesus became hungry, he fed them, even though there were five thousand

and he only had five barley loaves and two small fish. When Jesus needed money for his tax he told Peter to go catch a fish. In the mouth of the fish was enough money for all the disciples' tax. Again and again God provides for his people. Paul's argument is that He will not withhold anything from us after giving us Jesus His Son.

Romans 8:33 Who shall bring a charge against God's elect? It is God who justifies.

False charges, wrong charges, personal criticisms, slander, all wither in the burning light of imputed justification to the believer, you and me. When God justifies us, it manifests in our natural circumstances.

Daniel was charged with disobedience to the King. He had broken their law, yet he was delivered from the lion's den. God justified him. The evidence of him being right with God, justified in heaven was manifested on Earth. He was set free, and his enemies were given the same fate they attempted to bring on Daniel.

Joseph was charged with attempted rape. Yet, Joseph was justified by God, even though he was sent to prison, he was continually blessed. Eventually, in a single day, he was set free, making him the Prime Minister of the most powerful nation on Earth. When God justifies us, that rightness manifests in our circumstances. No matter how forcible the accusations are, God's justifying power is far more.

Romans 8:34 Who is he who condemns? It is Christ who

died, and furthermore is also risen, who is even at the right hand of God, who also makes intercession for us.

It is not Christ who condemns. Yet some, many, maybe even most, would easily imagine that Christ does condemn, because of the incredible number of individuals and organisations claiming to represent God yet seeking to lay guilt on people rather than releasing them from it. This is not a new situation. In the time of Jesus, the Pharisees were just as eager to burden the people with guilt rather than release them from it.

It would be unthinkable and absolutely ludicrous to imagine that Christ would go to the cross, suffer such an incredibly painful, degrading death in order to free us from the condemnation of God's justice, only to rise from the dead to accuse us of the very sins He died to set us free from! This is Paul's acutely powerful logic. Thus, we can definitely identify who the accuser is not! Sincere minds can easily imagine that it is God making them feel guilty, imagining that guilt, because it is a religious feeling, is originating in God. Nothing could be further from the truth. Guilt originates with the devil in hell. All the sicknesses, oppressions and other maladies of mankind ride on the heels of unreleased guilt. This is why Jesus settled for nothing less than a total release from sin.

Revelation 12:10 Then I heard a loud voice saying in heaven, 'Now salvation, and strength, and the kingdom of our God, and the power of His Christ have come, for the accuser of our brethren, who accused them before our God day and night, has been cast down.
11 And they overcame him by the blood of the Lamb and by the word of their testimony, and they did not love

their lives to the death.'

Salvation, power and the Kingdom is held back from Earth because the accuser, the devil has been able to keep a place in the 'heavenly' sphere. Everything in the natural world has its beginnings in the spiritual world. All that is visible begins in the invisible. Whatever is happening on Earth is a reflection of what is happening in the spiritual (the 'heavenly') world. If there is a blockage on Earth, we need to deal with that blockage in the heavenlies first. Ephesians 4:27 tells us to 'give no place to the devil'. Yet here we see that he did have a place, even surprisingly, in heaven. We give accusation a place when we believe it's from God. When we do not accept forgiveness, and imagine that remembering our sins and continually feeling bad about ourselves somehow pleases God, we are providing a place for the devil. One of the most effective blockages against God moving in the Earth is when the family of accusation is alive. This includes criticism, prejudice, judgment, blaming, guilt, condemnation and all those discouraging, strength sapping conditions that every believer struggles with at some point. Healing will not happen in an atmosphere of judgment. Deliverance from demons will not happen in an environment where blame is attributed to the sufferer. Freedom in the Holy Spirit will not happen in an environment of guilt. The greater the level of the absence of judgment, the greater will be the release of God's great power. Accepting our forgiveness and standing in our complete justification and the imputed perfect life of Jesus is essential for every believer if we are to overcome the devil and live in victory. Once the devil is cast down from that position of spiritual influence, Scripture tells us that a 'loud voice' declares that salvation, power and kingdom are 'now' released into the Earth. There isn't a true servant of God on Earth who isn't aching for lost people to be saved, for the power of God to manifest, and for the Kingdom of God to come in our churches and communities. The key to this release is removing accusation against the people of God. Our weapons are not human weapons but spiritual, and are extremely powerful in pulling down this stronghold of guilt over the church. The weapons we have been given are the blood of Jesus, speaking the Word of God and living unselfish lives. When we are prepared to pick up our cross and lay down our lives, lay claim to the power of the blood of Jesus, and speak the Word of God - we will find Satan's position weakened to the point where he loses his position in the spiritual realm and is cast down. Isaiah the prophet calls on us to condemn every tongue that rises against us in judgment. He assures us that there is no weapon devised against us that will prosper at all. The only answer to accusation is to cast it out. Any attempt to argue our own righteousness is futile. Arguing against our conscience, or against condemning thoughts will not succeed. There will always be something that is wrong. The Bible does not tell us to argue with the devil, only to resist him and he will flee. All accusations and condemnations are from the devil. None are from God. Resist every condemning thought. Cast them out, in the Name of Jesus.

Isaiah 54:17 No weapon formed against you shall prosper, and every tongue which rises against you in judgment you shall condemn. This is the heritage of the servants of the LORD, and their righteousness is from Me, says the LORD.

Our afterlife destination is no longer hell. It is heaven. We have been forgiven, justified, regenerated, adopted, sanctified and redeemed. Our admission to heaven is signed, sealed and delivered.

Instead of feeling shame over our mistakes and sins, Jesus has come into our lives to lift our heads in glory, not bow us down in shame.

> *Romans 8:30-31 Moreover whom He predestined, these He also called; whom He called, these He also justified; and whom He justified, these He also glorified. What then shall we say to these things? If God is for us, who can be against us?*

Recently I prepared a message titled, 'Lift up your eyes'. I was surprised how many times this phrase occurs in Scripture. Again and again the Lord told His people to lift up their eyes. In the light of how often, (almost every week), we are told to bow our heads and close our eyes in religious services, I wondered how many times that statement was in Scripture. Not once! Once or twice we are urged to bow down in worship, but certainly it is not meant to be the general posture of a child of God. Psalm 3:3 says God is the One who is my 'glory and the lifter of my head'. The Scripture above tells us we have been 'glorified'. This is the opposite of shamed. Jesus has not come into this world to shame us, causing us to bow our heads down. We have been lifted up with glory. This is not arrogance, but rather the synthesis of humility in accepting Christ as the source of all our glory, and the confidence in life of knowing who we are in Christ.

6. WE HAVE THE PROMISES OF GOD

2 Peter 1:4 ... by which have been given to us exceedingly great and precious promises, that through these you may be partakers of the divine nature, having escaped the corruption that is in the world through lust.

2 Corinthians 1:20 For all the promises of God in Him are Yes, and in Him Amen, to the glory of God through us.

Peter enlightens us as to why the promises of God exist. Firstly they are not simply to assure everyone of God's faithful love, which they do abundantly! They have been 'given to us' as part of our 'equipping' by which we appropriate the nature of God into our lives. We are meant to 'activate' the promises. The first step to this is by speaking them. The power of the promises is not just to bring comfort to troubled minds. The promises of God create realities that as yet do not exist in our circumstances. When we speak the promises of God we establish the covenant God has with us in this world.

When we speak the promises we release the power of God.

When we speak the promises, faith is born and strengthened within us.

When we speak the promises we defeat the devil. The Word is a sword.

When we speak the promises the Holy Spirit goes to work to fulfil the Word. God watches over His Word to perform it.

Even though we know that there is nothing God cannot do, there is one thing He is incapable of. He cannot lie. His Word is truth. We can trust His promises with our lives. Scripture contains thousands of promises from God to all of us. There is a promise from God for every situation we will ever face. We must know these promises, speaking them continually over our world.

7. WE HAVE FORGIVENESS

We are forgiven. Whether you feel it or not, from the moment you received Christ you received forgiveness from God. To receive Christ is to repent from the place where we did not have him in our lives, receive forgiveness and move into the freedom of a guiltless life.

Ephesians 1v7 In Him we have ... the forgiveness of sins.

Part of our covenant right in Christ is forgiveness. Forgiveness is something we 'have'. It's not something we are trying to obtain. It is part of our inheritance as sons and daughters of God. When we need forgiveness it is available. When we confess our sin we have forgiveness. It belongs to us. Thank God!

1John1v9 If we confess our sins, He is just and faithful to forgive us our sins and to cleanse us from all unrighteousness

One of the fundamental problems hindering us from experiencing forgiveness is our failure to forgive ourselves. Reliving the incident does not purge our soul from sin. Feeling bad about it will not do it. Only one entity has the power to cleanse the stain of sin from our soul, and that's the blood of

Jesus. The power of the blood of Jesus is activated when we believe we are forgiven. You say, 'But I don't feel forgiven'. The truth is however, that you are forgiven the moment you receive Christ and repent from sin. If this truth doesn't take root deep in a Christian's life they become dogged with condemnation all their life. Trying to be joyful and victorious while your conscience condemns you is impossible. Satan gains access to our minds through this weakness. Revelation 12 tells us the devil accuses us of our sins day and night, attempting to keep us discouraged and powerless. This will be our condition until we believe that the blood has cleansed us. This means we refuse to doubt that we are forgiven. We refuse to remember our sins, but rather we remember that we are the 'righteousness of God in Christ'.

2Co 5:21 For He made Him who knew no sin to be sin for us, that we might become the righteousness of God in Him.

The Word of God is 'seed' (Luke 8v11). This means that you can grow whatever you want in your life simply by planting the seed of that 'whatever' in your heart. If you want to grow apples in your garden, you don't plant pear seeds. If you are in need of the assurance of forgiveness, don't just meditate on anything in Scripture. Read what the Word of God declares about forgiveness. When you meditate in your mind on a specific 'seed' it digests in your soul. The light of its truth dawns in you like the morning sun. Faith comes by hearing the Word of God (Romans 10:13). Take a verse from the Bible that you are particularly attracted to, or need, on the subject and speak it. Faith will fill your heart. Use this faith to believe the scripture in an even more complete way. This is one of the most powerful spiritual cycles to be engaged in.

Isaiah 43v22-26 reveals that God is more interested in forgiving us than in remembering our sins. He tells us to FORGET the former things. **'Put Me in remembrance'**, He says. **'State your cause, that you may be acquitted'.**

The Lord wants you to win your case. Even though you are feeling conscience stricken, state your case, stand your ground that you have been forgiven through the blood of Jesus. Your sin may be serious, but Jesus' blood is far more serious. His power sets you completely free from all your sin. In the Old Testament, when the sinner brought a lamb as atonement for their sin, the priest did not look at the sins of the offerer. He looked at the lamb. God is looking at the sacrifice for your sin, Jesus. He is enough! He has completely covered us for the forgiveness of all our shortcomings.

8. WE HAVE JUSTIFICATION

We have justification. This is being 'declared righteous'. To be declared righteous is to be justified. The Greek word translated 'justify', means 'to declare righteous'. In Christ we have been declared righteous. Job asks the question;

> *Job 9v2 'How can a man be righteous (justified), before God?'*

Job's question is answered in Habakkuk 2:4, Romans 1:17

and Galatians 3:11. God saw that this truth is so vital it bears repeating three times in Scripture as a quote and then it is expounded time and again by Paul as he lays downs the doctrinal foundation for every believer and for the Church.

'The just shall live by faith'

The greatest problem Paul faced was migrating the conditions for salvation away from keeping the Law of Moses over to Christ. Under the Old Testament, the only way to be declared righteous was by being obedient to the Law of Moses. The only way to secure righteousness was to fully obey all that Law. This concept had been reinforced generation after generation. Now Paul faced the extraordinary challenge of tearing this down and replacing this enormous volume of requirements with the simplicity of receiving Christ! It was anathema to the traditional Hebrew. Paul persevered. In Romans 3:28 he declares;

> *'Therefore we conclude that a man is justified by faith apart from the deeds of the law'*

I'll say it again, 'to justify' is 'to declare righteous'. Jeremiah 23v6 reveals in capital letters that there will come a day when God will be known as;

'THE LORD OUR RIGHTEOUSNESS'

This is one of the names through which God is revealed in the Old Testament – 'Jehovah-Tsidkenu'. This name literally means, 'The Lord our righteousness'. This single statement contains one of the most illuminating revelations of salvation in the entire Bible. Not until the New Testament did the truth of it became fully understood. Paul continually reinforces that we are saved by grace, not our own merit. But how does grace accomplish this?

Christ lived a perfect human life. It was unblemished, unspotted, and unwrinkled by any sin or fault. He is the only person that has ever accomplished this. He was perfect in every respect. His thought life was perfect. His attitudes were perfect. His morals were above any reproach. His relationship with others was untarnished in any way. No part of His life offended God. He was the Son of God. Perfect. Following His ascension into Heaven, the Father reviewed His Son's life on Earth. It was perfectly perfect.

Jesus did not live His perfect life so it could be merely said, 'He lived a perfect life'. He did not live His life for himself. He lived His life for us. After dying as our sacrifice for sin, overcoming death and the devil, then ascending into heaven, He then proceeded to 'impute' this righteousness, His perfect life, to anyone who receives Him. Today, Christ's astonishing gift is His own righteousness imputed to our own account. We become right before God, not by our rightness, but by Christ's. It is His gift to us. His righteousness gains admission to heaven and access to eternity with God. The perfect life of Jesus Christ is deposited, as it were, to our account in heaven. His righteous life is now regarded as ours. God regards us as perfectly righteous, acquitted of all guilt and completely justified before Him! Gods own righteousness is imputed to us as becoming our own.

> *Romans 4v24 It (righteousness) shall be imputed to us who believe in Him who raised up Jesus our Lord from the dead.*

We now are able to stand before God with the same standing as Jesus Christ Himself.

As Job asked 'How should a man be righteous before God?' we could also ask 'How does a man believe God?' The answer to that question is the following;

> *Romans 10v6-10 The righteousness of faith speaks in this way... The word is near you, in your mouth and in your heart (that is the word of faith which we preach); that if you confess with your mouth the Lord Jesus and believe in your heart that God raised Him from the dead you shall be saved. For with the heart man believes unto righteousness and with the mouth confession is made unto salvation.*

Paul stated that he and his team preached the 'word of faith'. They preached the Word and by Paul's reckoning the Word created faith, not fear. The Word of God can be handled in a variety of ways, causing a variety of responses in the hearers. Some preach to bring fear, some, political points of view, some justice etc. Our highest calling in preaching is to bring faith into people's hearts. When people believe, they speak, and the words they speak are words of faith. This in turn causes faith to rise in the heart, and a positive cycle begins with one action influencing the other.

The heart is that part of our frame that believes. It's our

believing machine. This is the reason we need to guard it aggressively, because it can only be preoccupied with one major emotion at any given time. This is why Jesus regularly referred to our need to forgive whenever he spoke on prayer. Unforgiveness destroys the ability of the heart to believe, as does fear, hatred and anger. As we purge our hearts of these enemies each day through prayer, we bring ourselves to that place where we can believe. This is the fight of faith. It takes no effort to harbor negative emotions, but we need to be intentional if we are to build a heart filled with faith. A positive life doesn't happen by accident. It takes the same kind of effort as going to the gym every day to build a healthy, strong, toned body. As we take our mind and emotions through a workout every day, pushing against the things that resist a positive life, we will also build that strong inner person.

9. WE HAVE REGENERATION

The faith of our salvation experience must be built on what God says in His Word and not just our experience. Forgiveness has removed all that separated us from God. Alongside of this we are declared righteous, giving us rightness with God. We are on the same page as He is. We are fused together. This is eternal life. Through this fusion we are born again, regenerated. When we receive Christ we are born again.

> *John 1:12 But as many as received Him, to them He gave the right to become children of God, to those who believe in His name.*

The Bible describes this new birth in many ways. John says we are 'born again' (John 3:3); also translated as 'from above' (margin 3:3); John also describes this as 'born of God', (1John 5:1); and born of the Spirit (John 3:8); Peter says we are born of the incorruptible seed of the Word (1Peter 1:23); we are born not of blood, of flesh, or of the will of man, but by the will of God (John 1:13).

It seems obvious, but deserves to be stated because of the incredible reality – we have become the offspring of God Himself because He has given birth to us by His Spirit. Our entire nature is regenerated. We are 'babes' when we first enter the kingdom. This means we no longer 'try' to live as God wants us to. It becomes our nature to love, to be forgiving and joyful. These qualities belong to the believer by way of birth. We receive these because we are literally born of our Father in Heaven. This means the character and nature of God become imprinted into the inner template of the believer's mind, heart and soul. We bear the likeness and image of God. Regeneration is imperative to our salvation. We can now pray the Lord's prayer in reality instead of just a religious exercise; 'Our Father…' He is our Father because we have become His children, born of Him. God has no grandchildren. Every child of God is a direct son or daughter, born of Him. He does not become our grandfather, or uncle. He becomes our Father in Heaven. We carry the spiritual genetics of God our Father. This is where the 'gene' part of the word 're-gene-rated' is a reality. The seed of God grows within us the very nature of the Father.

Titus 3v5 He saved us, through the washing of regeneration, and renewing of the Holy Spirit.

The Holy Spirit is the One who is the essence of the new birth. However, regeneration is not the 'Baptism of the Holy Spirit', (which is a subsequent experience to being born again). When we accept the gift of salvation, the Father, the Son and the Holy Spirit come to dwell within us. Even so, we are yet to be 'endued' (clothed) with the power spoken of in Acts 2, when on the Day of Pentecost the disciples were baptized (soaked) in supernatural power.

Some groups have claimed that to be saved we must be baptized in the Holy Spirit. This is untrue. Speaking in tongues is evidence of being baptized in the Holy Spirit, not of being saved. Nowhere in scripture is there an adequate basis for the belief that one has to be 'baptized in the Holy Spirit' as the disciples were on the Day of Pentecost, to be saved.

On the other hand some claim we receive the baptism of the Holy Spirit at the point of the new birth, therefore there is no need to receive the baptism of the Holy Spirit at a separate and subsequent stage. This also is untrue. After the disciples were 'breathed on', by Jesus and told to 'receive the Holy Spirit' (John 20:22), they were then instructed to go to Jerusalem and wait for the promise of the Father which was the Baptism in the Holy Spirit, the clothing with power (Luke 24:49).

When we reach out in faith and ask Christ into out lives we are 'born' of the Holy Spirit into the kingdom.

John 1v12,13 But as many as received Him, to them He gave the right to become children of God, to those who believe in His Name; who were born, not of blood, nor of the will of the flesh, nor of the will of man, but of God'.

10. WE HAVE ADOPTION

Adoption was a legal process whereby a Roman citizen could transform a slave he 'owned' into a family member. After the price of citizenship was paid the adopted person also became a fully fledged Roman. This entitled him all the privileges denied non-Romans.

Adoption also raises the issue of choice. Adoption means the parent chooses the child. For most people, their parents planned their birth. Even then, parents have to accept 'whosoever' comes. The difference with those adopted is they have been handpicked.

> *Galatians 4:5 ... that we might receive the adoption of sons.*

The most immediate thought that follows sonship for Paul is inheritance. He continuously and consistently points out that if we are children of God, then we are heirs. Whether adopted or born, we become heirs of God.

> *Galatians 3:7 ... therefore you are no longer a slave but a son, and if a son, then an heir of God through Christ.*

Romans 8:17 ... if children then heirs - heirs of God and joint heirs with Christ.

All that Christ has inherited from the Father we also have inherited. We are joint heirs with Christ. Hebrews tells us that Jesus has inherited all things.

...His Son, whom He (God) has appointed heir of all things...

ALL THINGS. There is nothing that Christ has not inherited. This is all related to the fact that God has made us His children. On that basis we have become heirs - both in this life and in the one to come; **'of all things'**, because we have become joint inheritors of all that the Father has prepared.

11. WE HAVE SANCTIFICATION

Being in Christ is being set apart. The word translated sanctification is the same one used for holy. It comes from the root word 'hagios'. It describes what consecration, sacredness, purity, and holiness is. It is also translated 'to set apart'. This means it is set apart for sacred use. When you are saved, God sanctifies you. He sets you apart from this world for His exclusive use. You are consecrated to Him. Paul tells the Romans to yield to this truth and actively give themselves wholly to God in a 'sanctified' lifestyle.

Romans 12v1 I beseech you therefore brethren by the mercies of God that you present your bodies a living sacrifice, holy, acceptable to God, which is your reasonable service.

This is our 'reasonable' response to all that God has made us 'in Christ'. Some people think that they need to become holy to get saved. Wrong! We get saved and then we are made holy by God's divine fiat. Once we receive Christ He works from the basis that we are in Him and therefore already declared holy. A fish isn't gutted before it's caught! Our entire pilgrimage on Earth is to outwork what Christ has worked in us. Our natural self and circumstances conforms to the finished salvation we already have within us. Our sanctification was complete, the moment we received Christ.

> *1 Corinthians 6v11 But you were washed, but you were sanctified, but you were justified in the name of the Lord Jesus and by the Spirit of our God.*

> *1 Corinthians 1v30 ...you are in Christ Jesus, who became for us...righteousness and sanctification, and redemption.*

Throughout the New Testament, believers are called 'saints'. As we have already covered, the tradition of making a person a saint after they have died is a religious tradition with no basis in Scripture. However, God has no difficulty in calling us who are alive in Him, 'saints'. This is because He has 'made' us so. By an act of the Holy Spirit we are sanctified. In the Old Testament, priests, prophets, Kings, people, temples, sacred clothing and instruments were all anointed with oil when they were set apart for God. They were thus considered 'holy'.

In the New Testament the oil is the Holy Spirit. When we are born again by the Holy Spirit He comes to dwell in us. He accomplishes the work of sanctification. This work resonates in the heart of any truly born again person. They immediately turn their back on the world. The fruit of being sanctified is a love for purity, holiness and the presence of God. This quest for purity becomes a lifelong pursuit as we wrestle with all the opposing allurements and temptations of the world and our flesh.

We don't get holy so we can receive the Holy Spirit. The 'way' of God is to pour His Spirit upon us by grace and He, the Spirit, makes us holy. Being holy is basically being set apart from this world unto God. Holiness is being cleansed from the uncleanness of this world, and being set aside exclusively for God. You are sanctified. You are holy, declared to be so by the Father Himself.

12. WE HAVE REDEMPTION

Ephesians 1v7 In Him we have redemption through His blood.

Redemption means 'to buy back'. The Greek word 'apolutrosis' used for 'ransom' is translated 'redemption' in the New Testament. Another Greek Word, 'lutron', is also used for redemption. This has the meaning of, 'to set something free, with a redemption price'. The picture is of a slave in the slave market having their freedom purchased by someone else. They are 'set free', through being bought at the market price then freed by the purchaser.

A truer picture of our state is if we understand the slave is the son of the purchaser. Somehow over the years the son drifted from his home, and found himself caught in a crime. Unable to pay the fine he has to sell himself as a slave in order to cover the debt. The Father saw his own child, you and me, bound by sin, a slave to sin. The law demanded that the price of freeing a slave was the price of a man. The Father, out of deep love for his child, paid whatever the price required by law. He sent His only begotten Son, Christ, to pay the price of our freedom from slavery. We have been bought back by the price of Christ's life. His shed blood is evidence the price has been paid.

It could also be seen like a young boy who builds a model yacht. He takes it to the river and sets it sailing. A gust of wind catches the little boat. It sails away too fast for the lad to keep up. It disappears far in the distance. The boy searches for it day after day with no joy. His boat has been lost. Some time later in a distant town he passes a pawnshop where he sees his lost yacht sitting in the window. He goes to the counter and tells the shopkeeper that he is the owner of the boat in the window. The shopkeeper tells him he is wrong. He is the owner, now. Someone sold it to him. The boy asks how he can recover the boat. The answer is obvious. Purchase it. The boy finds the money, pays the man and walks away with the boat he purchased. He redeemed his boat. It is something he has 'bought back'.

This leads to the next powerful concept, that we are now the possession of God. We are His property. He paid the price for us. We now belong to Him. Our lives and circumstance need to now glorify God.

> *1Corinthians 6v19,20'...you are not your own, for you were bought at a price, therefore glorify God in your body and in your spirit which are God's'.*

Our faith is strong when we realize that we are God's property. He has assumed the responsibility for our lives. He has taken it on Himself to take care of us and ensure that His property is well catered for. He has purchased us, redeemed us from the hand of the devil, from the power of sin, and from judgment itself.

Our faith in God is strong when it's born of revelation from God's Word rather than just our own thoughts and feelings, which will follow faith when we choose to believe the Word. Our feelings will demand attention and seem to be our reality, however, if we place our faith in them, we will inevitably stumble. Faith in His promises assures us of victory. If we interpret God's attitude towards us through our feelings or circumstances instead of the Word, we will live a very insecure life. The Word of God 'changes not'. Same with the Father. Not even a 'shadow of turning'. He and His Word are unchanging. Our faith must be in His Word and not our feelings, which have no authority whatsoever to dictate to us what the reality of life is. Feelings are powerful and important but not enough to usurp the supremacy of God's Word over our lives.

13. WE HAVE AN INHERITANCE

Paul argues convincingly and through the inspiration of the

Holy Spirit, that because we are children of God we are now also heirs alongside Jesus.

> *Rom 8:16, 17 The Spirit Himself bears witness with our spirit that we are children of God, and if children, then heirs—heirs of God and joint heirs with Christ.*

Question - Is the inheritance for this life or the next?
Answer - Both.
Question - What then, is our inheritance in this life?
Answer - The world.

> *Romans 4:13 For the promise that he would be the HEIR OF THE WORLD was not to Abraham or to his seed through the law, but through the righteousness of faith.*

This is possibly both one of the most overlooked and most amazing Scriptures at the same time. This is saying that the Israelites, the descendants of Abraham were only promised the land of Canaan, but it was God's intention for them to take the entire globe. The promise to Abraham and his seed was that he, and therefore his seed, would inherit the world! The New Testament clearly states that we are now considered Abraham's seed and therefore heirs of the same promises he received. We are the God-ordained heirs of the world.

On top of that, the blessing God pronounced on Abraham is also pronounced on us. Whatever blessings were upon him are now upon you and me on the basis that Christ is in our lives. See these Scriptures which outline the blessing that God placed upon Abraham.

Gen 12:2 I will make you a great nation; I will bless you and make your name great; and you shall be a blessing. 3 I will bless those who bless you, and I will curse him who curses you; and in you all the families of the earth shall be blessed.

Gen 17:4 As for Me, behold, My covenant is with you, and you shall be a father of many nations.

Gen 22:17 blessing I will bless you, and in multiplying I will multiply your descendants as the stars of the heaven and as the sand which is on the seashore; and your descendants shall possess the gate of their enemies.

Gen 28:14 Also your descendants shall be as the dust of the earth; you shall spread abroad to the west and the east, to the north and the south; and in you and in your seed all the families of the earth shall be blessed.

This is the list of blessings the great patriarch obtained from God, not just for himself but for all those who are his seed.

I will make you a **great nation**
I will **bless you**
I will make **your name great**
You shall **be a blessing**
I will **bless those who bless you**
I will **curse him who curses you**
In you **all the families of the Earth will be blessed**
My covenant is with you
You shall **father many nations**

I will **multiply you** as the stars and as the sand
Your descendants will **overpower their enemies**
You shall spread to the North, South, East, West

Christ in us is the basis for claiming a right to this inheritance.

> *Galatians 3:29 And if you are Christ's, then YOU ARE ABRAHAM'S SEED, and heirs according to the promise.*

> *Hebrews 11:9 By faith he dwelt in the land of promise as in a foreign country, dwelling in tents with ISAAC and Jacob, the HEIRS WITH HIM OF THE SAME PROMISE.*

> *Galatians 4:28 NOW WE, brethren, AS ISAAC WAS, ARE CHILDREN OF PROMISE.*

This means that in exactly the same way as Isaac was an heir of the promises upon Abraham his father, so we now are also inheritors of the same promise.

Obviously our inheritance extends beyond this world into the next. However, whenever that is emphasized, I find people tend to dismiss the blessings God has promised us in this life as though they were unimportant and so much lesser than spiritual and eternal blessings. I get the feeling people are wanting to impress themselves and others with their spiritual sincerity as though to not be blessed in this life is more holy and pleasing to the Father. We are destined by God to enjoy His blessing in this life and in the next.

14. WE HAVE BLESSING

Ephesians 1:3 Blessed be the God and Father of our Lord Jesus Christ, who has blessed us with every spiritual blessing in the heavenly places in Christ.

We are now blessed and not cursed. We are blessed with every spiritual blessing there is. These blessings are not yet to come, or even falling on us at present. We already have been blessed if we are in Christ. No curse has any power anymore to block the blessing of God upon us.

Galations 3:13 Christ has redeemed us from the curse of the law, having become a curse for us (for it is written, 'Cursed is everyone who hangs on a tree')

The curse of the law is outlined in Leviticus 26 and Deuteronomy 28, and makes for hair-raising reading. Obedience to the law meant incredible blessing, yet disobedience brought astonishing judgment. The terrible point about the law is that it was impossible to keep, (according to Paul) so therefore the curses of these two passages are inevitable for those who do not know the Lord. The curse brought terrible catastrophes upon the circumstances of those affected. The death of Jesus disabled the power of these curses. No curse has any effect on the life of the believer whatsoever.

Because the curse has been removed, instead of being cursed we are now blessed! This means that life in the city will be blessed, not cursed. The market place, the entertainment, the justice systems, the education, the hospitals, the religious establishments, the transport and communications, the media, the sporting world, the industries, the finances, the banking systems, the housing; the whole of the circumstances of the city will be blessed. Likewise the countryside, all of the grain crops, the dairy produce, the animal farms, the rivers, the rainfall, the seed for planting, the harvesting, the weather, the health of the crops and the animals, all will come under the blessing instead of the curse.

We can now expect every one of the curses threatened to those who did not keep Moses' law to be reversed.

Deuteronomy 28:17 Cursed shall be your basket and your kneading bowl.

This meant that whatever was taken in the field for preparation in the house would either not be enough, or be of poor quality. The kneading bowl would not bring enough dough for cooking to satisfy the family. The food preparation would be insufficient or else the food would taste terrible and have little nourishment. But now because Christ has sacrificed his life to remove the curse, we are blessed with more than enough. All the food is blessed. It tastes great and there is an abundance.

Deuteronomy 28:18 Cursed shall be the fruit of your body and the produce of your land, the increase of your cattle and the offspring of your flocks.

Your sons and daughters would bring you trouble and difficulty. They would be a curse to you instead of a blessing. That is, if you managed to even have children, because the curse would descend on the womb and render it barren. Even the produce of the land would not reproduce. It would fail to give you seed to sow for next year's crop. Your cattle and sheep would not reproduce. They would be barren, and what they do bring forth would be so inferior it will useless for selling or even useful for farming.

But now, because Christ has died, these curses are removed. Our sons and daughters will be a blessing. Couples unable to have children will have them. There will not only be enough there will be an abundance left over. There will not just be a maintaining of what exists, but there will be unending increase of the blessing upon people's lives, because of the work of the Cross.

> *Deuteronomy 28:19 Cursed shall you be when you come in, and cursed shall you be when you go out.*

Under the curse when you came into the house, things would go wrong and homecoming would not be pleasant. Your house would not be a refuge. It would be a place you want to get away from. Even when you went out things would go wrong. The car would break down. Accidents would happen. You may have planned to have a good time, but it would be miserable, because it would not go as you hoped. It would be awful. You would get fines for parking in the wrong spot. People would steal things from your home and you would wish you hadn't gone out.

But now, when we receive Christ, the good news is that the curse is removed. Coming home is beautiful. Your home is a refuge. Your car works well. When you go out you have a good time. Protection covers your home, and your belongings. Even if things do go wrong they will be forced to turn out for the best because there is no curse on you, rather the blessing of God.

> *Deuteronomy 28:20 The LORD will send on you cursing, confusion, and rebuke in all that you set your hand to do, until you are destroyed and until you perish quickly, because of the wickedness of your doings in which you have forsaken Me.*

Under the curse you would be confused and not know what to do. You would seek guidance and get none. You would try to make decisions but never feel confident about anything. You would attempt to start a business and although you might have had all the statistics saying it would go well, it would not because of the curse and rebuke from God upon all that you set your hand to.

But now, because the curse is gone, so has confusion. You are set free to make clear minded decisions. Even a little effort is rewarded in a big way. Because the blessing rests on you, you make strong, good decisions and they work well.

> *Deuteronomy 28:21 The LORD will make the plague cling to you until He has consumed you from the land which you are going to possess.*

> *Deuteronomy 28:22 The LORD will strike you with consumption, with fever, with inflammation, with severe burning fever, with the sword, with scorching, and with*

mildew; they shall pursue you until you perish.

Under the curse physical sicknesses would cling to you, and would not go away. It would literally cling to you even though you take all kinds of medication to make it go away. Some of the sicknesses that would cling include *'consumption'*, which has been identified as pulmonary tuberculosis - *phthisis* or as the side effects of wasting and emaciation from prolonged bouts of malarial fever - some have even suggested cancer; *'fever'*, refers to any number of diseases: malaria, typhoid, typhus, dysentery, chronic diarrhea, or cholera.; *'inflammation'*, when injury becomes worse rather than better and the healing processes of the body fail, or become infected; *'the sword'*, refers to being struck by the sword and wounded by the effects of war; *'scorching and mildew'*, refers to drought and diseases that would come upon the crops of Israel so that they would fail to come to fruit. All these would follow after the Israelites because of the curse of the law, *'until they would perish'*.

But now, Christ absorbed the curse in His body and then killed it through His death. All these terrible plagues have no part in you. Neither sickness, nor war, nor plagues upon people and crops will fall on you. Others may get sick with these things, but they will avoid you. They won't rest on you because you are under the blessing, not the curse.

> *Deuteronomy 28:23 And your heavens which are over your head shall be bronze, and the earth which is under you shall be iron.*
> *Deuteronomy 28:24 The LORD will change the rain of your land to powder and dust; from the heaven it shall come down on you until you are destroyed.*

Under the curse drought would ravage the land so that the earth became as hard as iron and dust would cover the sky rather than rain; *'until destruction comes'*.

But now, when a nation embraces Christ as it's Savior, the curse is broken and the blessing of God overtakes all the curses, breaking the worst of conditions - in this case, for an agricultural community, drought.

> *Deuteronomy 28:25 The LORD will cause you to be defeated before your enemies; you shall go out one way against them and flee seven ways before them; and you shall become troublesome to all the kingdoms of the earth.*
>
> *Deuteronomy 28:26 Your carcasses shall be food for all the birds of the air and the beasts of the earth, and no one shall frighten them away.*

Under the curse, instead of defeating your enemies, they would defeat you. Notice the Word says you will have enemies. This can't be avoided. Under the curse you would be defeated by them, but under the blessing you would triumph over them. Under the curse you would flee from the opposition. Under blessing they flee from you. Under the curse you would not be favored by the nations, but rather be considered a nuisance to the nations of the Earth. The people of the Earth would be happy to see you destroyed by the birds and beasts. Under the blessing of God the church needs to accept that they are the light for this world, they hold the answer. Instead, often the church has been considered a nuisance, something people see no value for.

Deuteronomy 28:27 The LORD will strike you with the boils of Egypt, with tumors, with the scab, and with the itch, from which you cannot be healed.
Deuteronomy 28:28 The LORD will strike you with madness and blindness and confusion of heart.

Under the curse, the sicknesses of the world come upon you; the *boils* - a general Bible term to describe inflamed swellings of the skin; the Hebrew word literally means ulcers; *tumors* - a disease most commentators find difficult to identify yet agree is regarded as fatal; the *scab* and the *itch* - which refers to skin diseases such as eczema, leprosy, scales and ringworm. Incurable diseases were predicted to be part of the curse. Insanity, blindness and confusion would also come upon those that were under the curse of the law.

But now with the curse removed, the sicknesses of the world have no access into our lives. Because of the blessing of God, we will be struck with good health, and healing of any illness that may happen. We will be struck with sanity, vision, and peace in our hearts.

Deuteronomy 28:29 And you shall grope at noonday, as a blind man gropes in darkness; you shall not prosper in your ways; you shall be only oppressed and plundered continually, and no one shall save you.

Under the curse you are overcome by oppressors and those who wished to take advantage of you. You would be 'ripped off' again and again and wonder why. The curse of the law rests upon the person who has not received Christ. Generally there is at least someone who will seek to help the unfortunate out of their plight, but not so under these conditions. No one will come to your aid.

But now because this curse is also removed, we will be released from things that bind us, set free from oppressors, and instead of being taken advantage of, we will be blessed with great deals, enormous bargains, incredible bonuses. If we do find ourselves in difficulty, people will come to our aid and help us get out of the problem.

Deuteronomy 28:30   You shall betroth a wife, but another man shall lie with her; you shall build a house, but you shall not dwell in it; you shall plant a vineyard, but shall not gather its grapes.

Deuteronomy 28:31   Your ox shall be slaughtered before your eyes, but you shall not eat of it; your donkey shall be violently taken away from before you, and shall not be restored to you; your sheep shall be given to your enemies, and you shall have no one to rescue them.

Deuteronomy 28:32   Your sons and your daughters shall be given to another people, and your eyes shall look and fail with longing for them all day long; and there shall be no strength in your hand.

Deuteronomy 28:33   A nation whom you have not known shall eat the fruit of your land and the produce of your labor, and you shall be only oppressed and crushed continually.

Deuteronomy 28:34   So you shall be driven mad because of the sight which your eyes see.

Under the curse all security departs from you. Another person would sleep with your wife. You would build your own home, but not live in it. For one reason or another, someone else would live in the house you thought you were building for yourself. You would start a business but someone else would buy it out and reap all the benefits of it. This is the curse of the law. You work hard at obtaining and creating something but others reap the benefits. All your inventions, hard work and efforts would reap nothing because others would take away your employees, your management team, your workers and your clients - all would be taken from you. Your children would depart from you and your heart will break over longing for them to be with you, yet you would not have any ability to win them back. Strangers, not even family or friends would eat and enjoy all the hard work you've put in. All these conditions would produce instability of mind, as a certain kind of madness would set in.

But now, in Christ, under the blessing of God, free from the curse through the death of Jesus, your spouse will remain faithful, the home and business you build will be blessed, and you will eat the fruit of your labor. Clients, employees, family members, will be loyal to you. You will enjoy great peace of mind as you and your family and your friends enjoy the blessing of Heaven.

> *Deuteronomy 28:35 The LORD will strike you in the knees and on the legs with severe boils which cannot be healed, and from the sole of your foot to the top of your head.*

These sound like the kind of boils Job had, which have been identified with smallpox or with treponematosis (a parasitic infection.)

Under the blessing of God the only thing that is going to strike you is healing and health, again and again, and again.

> *Deuteronomy 28:36 The LORD will bring you and the king whom you set over you to a nation which neither you nor your fathers have known, and there you shall serve other gods; wood and stone.*

The worst thing about these curses is that the glory of God would no longer be among you, but rather the lifeless gods of mere wood and stone, which give no glory at all to those who serve them. You would be transported out of the kingdom of God into a strange land, where you would have no friends, but only strangers.

Maybe the greatest blessing we can know, set free from the curse, is the presence of God in our lives, at home, at work, in the car, on holiday, in family life, in solitary life. God is with us. This is the greatest blessing of the New Testament. This is the greatest reason for which Jesus suffered the death He did. To connect us with His Father, and to remain in fellowship with Him.

> *Deuteronomy 28:37 And you shall become an astonishment, a proverb, and a byword among all nations where the LORD will drive you.*

Under the curse respect is lost and instead, mockery is inherited. The inhabitants of the lands to which you would be sent would hate you. People would make fun of you, and joke about you.

But now, in Christ, under the blessing of God the people of God are respected, even feared. They become the most prosperous people, they enjoy influence and leadership through natural and supernatural means. Their words come to pass. Their practical compassion makes them valued above all others in the community. Their servanthood makes them indispensable. The acts of God accompanying them bring awe and reverence for them.

> *Deuteronomy 28:38 You shall carry much seed out to the field but gather little in, for the locust shall consume it.*
> *Deuteronomy 28:39 You shall plant vineyards and tend them, but you shall neither drink of the wine nor gather the grapes; for the worms shall eat them.*
> *Deuteronomy 28:40 You shall have olive trees throughout all your territory, but you shall not anoint yourself with the oil; for your olives shall drop off.*
> *Deuteronomy 28:41 You shall beget sons and daughters, but they shall not be yours; for they shall go into captivity.*
> *Deuteronomy 28:42 Locusts shall consume all your trees and the produce of your land.*

Under the curse all your efforts to produce crops, build businesses, plant orchards, raise stock would fail because of diseases, and insects that would destroy them. Even your sons and daughters would be of no value to you, but rather a grief because strangers would steal them away into slavery and captivity.

But now free from the curse, your seed will produce the maximum possible, your harvest will come in, your business will grow, your stock will increase. Your sons and daughters will be of benefit to you, not just a burden. You will not be so burdened with debt and trying to make ends meet. The blessing upon you will accelerate your earning ability, increase your business, and multiply the results.

> *Deuteronomy 28:43 The alien who is among you shall rise higher and higher above you, and you shall come down lower and lower.*
> *Deuteronomy 28:44 He shall lend to you, but you shall not lend to him; he shall be the head, and you shall be the tail.*
> *Under the curse those who are strangers and foreigners amongst you in your own land and your own houses would rise up to rule over you in civic government areas, financial areas, business, entertainment, sports and education, so that you are servile to them. They would lend money to you and you would be 'wagged' like the tail, whilst they were the head.*
> *But now because you're in Christ and His work on the cross has obliterated the curse of the law, you will rise, in humility, higher and higher. The power of 'lift' will be in you. Instead of you seeking money from the world, the world will be seeking money from you. You will gain the control and the power of direction - as in being the head, and not the tail. The blessing of God brings the power of influence, so that society is changed by the people of God. This comes because they gain power through financial abundance, or through being elevated to positions of*

power. Under the curse we lose these. Under the blessing they become gifts from God.

Deuteronomy 28:45 Moreover all these curses shall come upon you and pursue and overtake you, until you are destroyed.
Deuteronomy 28:46 And they shall be upon you for a sign and a wonder, and on your descendants forever.
Deuteronomy 28:47 Because you did not serve the LORD your God with joy and gladness of heart, for the abundance of everything,
Deuteronomy 28:48 therefore you shall serve your enemies, whom the LORD will send against you, in hunger, in thirst, in nakedness, and in need of everything; and He will put a yoke of iron on your neck until He has destroyed you.

Because of your disobedience to the Lord, these curses would eventually overwhelm and destroy you, until you were in slavery to foreigners and in abject poverty: in need of everything.

But now, in Christ, under the blessing of God the curses are lifted off us so there is not one left. We serve the Lord with joy and gladness of heart, and instead of hunger and thirst and nakedness, we are filled with good food, and drink, and clothed with best clothes. We find ourselves in need of nothing.

Deuteronomy 28:49 The LORD will bring a nation against you from afar, from the end of the earth, as swift as the eagle flies, a nation whose language you will not understand,

Deuteronomy 28:50   a nation of fierce countenance, which does not respect the elderly nor show favor to the young.

Deuteronomy 28:51   And they shall eat the increase of your livestock and the produce of your land, until you are destroyed; they shall not leave you grain or new wine or oil, or the increase of your cattle or the offspring of your flocks, until they have destroyed you.

Deuteronomy 28:52   They shall besiege you at all your gates until your high and fortified walls, in which you trust, come down throughout all your land; and they shall besiege you at all your gates throughout all your land which the LORD your God has given you.

Deuteronomy 28:53   You shall eat the fruit of your own body, the flesh of your sons and your daughters whom the LORD your God has given you, in the siege and desperate straits in which your enemy shall distress you.

Deuteronomy 28:54   The sensitive and very refined man among you will be hostile toward his brother, toward the wife of his bosom, and toward the rest of his children whom he leaves behind,

Deuteronomy 28:55   so that he will not give any of them the flesh of his children whom he will eat, because he has nothing left in the siege and desperate straits in which your enemy shall distress you at all your gates.

Deuteronomy 28:56   The tender and delicate woman among you, who would not venture to set the sole of her foot on the ground because of her delicateness and sensitivity, will refuse to the husband of her bosom, and to her son and her daughter,

Deuteronomy 28:57 her placenta which comes out from between her feet and her children whom she bears; for she will eat them secretly for lack of everything in the siege and desperate straits in which your enemy shall distress you at all your gates.

Because of the curse merciless, fierce enemies would come against you who would completely destroy you and besiege you to the point where you would be debased to do terrible things even to your own family, such as destroying your own children.

But now under the blessing you are free from the victory of enemies. If they do attack, they will not win. Your cities, houses and families will be secure. Instead, your children grow up, developed to their full potential, blessed in every way.

Deuteronomy 28:58 If you do not carefully observe all the words of this law that are written in this book, that you may fear this glorious and awesome name, THE LORD YOUR GOD,

Deuteronomy 28:59 then the LORD will bring upon you and your descendants extraordinary plagues; great and prolonged plagues; and serious and prolonged sicknesses.

Plagues that have never even been heard of would come upon those who have this curse upon them. They would last for extraordinarily long times, be unusually large, and be of such an unusual nature there would be no cure for them.

But now, in Christ, under the blessing of God, you will

be set free from plagues that are attacking everyone else. If you do get sick, it will not last long. You will get over illness quickly.

Deuteronomy 28:60 Moreover He will bring back on you all the diseases of Egypt, of which you were afraid, and they shall cling to you.
Deuteronomy 28:61 Also every sickness and every plague, which is not written in this Book of the Law, will the LORD bring upon you until you are destroyed.
Deuteronomy 28:62 You shall be left few in number, whereas you were as the stars of heaven in multitude, because you would not obey the voice of the LORD your God.

Under the curse you would become pathetically few in number rather than a vast multitude, and therefore your power, nobility, and strength amongst others would become nothing.
But now because we are set free form the curse, the church will increase more and more throughout the whole Earth. Under the blessing we will outstrip the numbers of people who are not saved in our world.

Deuteronomy 28:63 And it shall be, that just as the LORD rejoiced over you to do you good and multiply you, so the LORD will rejoice over you to destroy you and bring you to nothing; and you shall be plucked from off the land which you go to possess.

Under the curse, God Himself would be happy to destroy

you because you were such an offence and grief to Him.
He would cause you to be removed from your homeland
where all your fond memories, family relationships, and
possessions were. You would be sent to a land where you
have no history or sense of belonging.
But now, in Christ and set free from the curse, God's
only joy is to see you happy, blessed and living in victory.
His great joy is to multiply you and do you good. His
determination is that you dwell safely in the land.

Deuteronomy 28:64 Then the LORD will scatter you
among all peoples, from one end of the earth to the other,
and there you shall serve other gods, which neither you
nor your fathers have known; wood and stone.
Deuteronomy 28:65 And among those nations you shall
find no rest, nor shall the sole of your foot have a resting
place; but there the LORD will give you a trembling
heart, failing eyes, and anguish of soul.
Deuteronomy 28:66 Your life shall hang in doubt before
you; you shall fear day and night, and have no assurance
of life.
Deuteronomy28:67 In the morning you shall say, 'Oh,
that it were evening!' And at evening you shall say, 'Oh,
that it were morning!' because of the fear which terrifies
your heart, and because of the sight which your eyes see.

Under the curse you would experience restlessness, anxiety
and never enjoy security, stability or peacefulness. Your heart
would be anxious and panic stricken as you were without
vision for the future. Your soul would be in pain and anguish.
You would be doubtful about whether or not you are going to

live, and yet you would never feel safe about your well-being. You would wish that your life was over and that your days would be numbered, so that you no longer experience the terror and fear of your life.

But now, in Christ, free from this curse, you are secure, safe, restful, not restless. Your life will not be in doubt, but you will completely assured of the blessing. Instead of fear filling your heart, faith will overwhelm all your doubts. The vision you have of the future will cause you to be inspired and enthused with fresh energy.

> *Deuteronomy 28:68 And the LORD will take you back to Egypt in ships, by the way of which I said to you, 'You shall never see it again.' And there you shall be offered for sale to your enemies as male and female slaves, but no one will buy you.*

Under the curse you would be taken back to places you never wanted to return to. Your whole life would seem to go backwards, and there you would try to at least eke out a living - but no one would want you or employ you. The final and most terrible thing would be that you were rejected and not wanted by anybody.

But now, in Christ, under the blessing of God, you progress. You move forward. You will not be trying to sell yourself to others to make some money. Instead you will be employing all sorts of people. You will be the one calling the shots.

If Jesus has died to remove the curse then **that is what has happened.** The curse has been removed.

For a curse to be effective it must have grounds for resting on someone's life. Once the blood of Christ has washed all sins from our soul, there remains no more ground for any curse whatsoever to gain access to our world.

> *Proverbs 26:2 Like a flitting sparrow, like a flying swallow, So a curse without cause shall not alight.*

This means that all those curses have been removed and reversed, so that under the blessing of God, instead of curses, blessings shower down on our lives in all these same areas.

15. WE HAVE AUTHORITY OVER THE DEVIL

How many Christians constantly complain about the devil attacking them? They seem to be completely overrun by devils assailing them all the time. This is not the position of a New Testament believer. Paul tells us **we've been set free** from the devil through the work of the cross.

> *Colossians 2:15 Having disarmed principalities and powers, He made a public spectacle of them, triumphing over them in it.*

This refers to the fact that Jesus has defeated the devil, in hell, and publicly displayed this fact to every demon in the realms of darkness. The conflict Jesus had with the devil was predicted right from the start in the garden of Eden.

> *Genesis 3:15 And I will put enmity between you and the*

woman, And between your seed and her Seed; He shall bruise your head, And you shall bruise His heel.

This prophecy declared there was to be a battle where the devil would bruise the heel of Jesus, but Jesus would bruise the head of Satan. This means Jesus brought His heel down heavily on the head of the devil. For that to happen the devil had to be on the ground, defeated in a battle.

David also prophesied that Jesus would take captives in His ascension from the grave.

> *Psalm 68:18 When you ascended on high, you led captives in your train;*

Isaiah also predicted the battle Jesus has to have and that the spoils of His victory would be shared.

> *Isaiah 53:12 Therefore I will give him a portion among the great, and he will divide the spoils with the strong, because he poured out his life unto death, and was numbered with the transgressors. For he bore the sin of many, and made intercession for the transgressors.*

Jesus Himself revealed the principle by which He releases people from the grip of Satan. He will first bind the devil, then He will take those who have been held captive.

> *Matthew 12:29 Or again, how can anyone enter a strong man's house and carry off his possessions unless he first ties up the strong man? Then he can rob his house.*

Luke 11:22 But when someone stronger attacks and overpowers him, he takes away the amour in which the man trusted and divides up the spoils.

Jesus realized he had to both bind the 'strongman', as well as remove all the armory before He could take his possessions.

When Jesus died, He first went to the presence of God, then went into the regions of hell where He entered into a conflict with the devil. When Peter says that Jesus 'preached' to the spirits (1 Peter 3:9), the word used 'kerusso', means to herald as a Public Crier. This was the person who announced news that affected everyone in a town. A trumpeter sounded to gain the attention of the people, then a royal proclamation, or whatever else, would be shouted out by the town crier. In the absence of radio, television, fax, telephone, computers, this was the only method of speaking to a large number of people at any given time.

After Jesus defeated Satan in an enormous battle in hell, He made a spectacle of the devil to all the demons and angels. He paraded the devil defeated, bound, hobbled and stripped of authority. He led the devil past all the cohorts of the evil one in the corridors of Hades. Then Jesus announced to all the devils in hell that His name was Jesus Christ and that he now held the keys to hell and death, and that whenever any demon heard His name spoken by someone in Christ, they must bow the knee and obey.

Philippians 2:10 that at the name of Jesus every knee should bow, of those in heaven, and of those on earth, and of those under the earth.

His 'preaching', was the proclamation of His victory. After three days Jesus rose victorious, having utterly disarmed the devil (Colossians 2:15). All the weapons and amour that the devil trusted in, was stripped from him. The power of sin was completely annihilated through the blood of Christ. Because Jesus fulfilled and superseded the law, the devil could not accuse people by means of the law. The grounds for any accusation against a person were taken away through Christ bringing forgiveness, acceptance and justification through the work of the cross. The power of death, sickness, and sin was removed from the devil as the pure, spotless Christ of Heaven could not be contained in hell (Acts 2:24). The only legal foothold the devil has for access and control over humans is sin. Sin is his doorway into the human soul. But Jesus slammed the door shut in the devil's face when he removed sin through the cross. Satan no longer has any means to gain access into a person's life when they are in Christ. The benefits of the cross obviously only apply if we have received Christ. The Believers Study Bible says of Colossians 2:15, that the 'public display' Jesus made of the devil was a picture drawn from the triumphant Roman general who would strip his foes and lead them as captives behind his chariot in a victory procession through the streets of Rome before the Caesar. The captured foes and all their nobles were often stripped naked and hobbled, shuffling along behind the chariot of the victorious general, so their humiliation, disarmament and powerlessness was complete.

16. WE HAVE PROSPERITY

Galatians 4:28 Now we, brethren, as Isaac was, are children of promise.

What kind of blessing did Isaac actually enjoy then?

Genesis 26:12-14 Then Isaac sowed in that land, and reaped in the same year a hundredfold; and the LORD blessed him.
13 The man began to prosper, and continued prospering until he became very prosperous;
14 for he had possessions of flocks and possessions of herds and a great number of servants. So the Philistines envied him.

Prosperity then for the people of God is His intention.

3 John 1:2 Beloved, I pray that you may prosper in all things and be in health, just as your soul prospers.

Psalms 35:27 Let them shout for joy and be glad, who favor my righteous cause; and let them say continually, 'Let the LORD be magnified, who has pleasure in the prosperity of His servant.'

2 Corinthians 8:9 For you know the grace of our Lord Jesus Christ, that though He was rich, yet for your sakes He became poor, that you through His poverty might become rich.

Paul is here referring to the fact that Jesus Christ died without one possession to his name, without one stitch of clothing on His body, without any money at all - so that he could take poverty to the cross and secure its defeat for those who embrace the Savior.

This Scripture is couched right in the middle of two Chapters written to the Corinthians dealing almost exclusively with the subject of money. Many commentators have great difficulty admitting that this passage is actually dealing with money. In fact I don't think I've yet found one who agrees that Paul is speaking specifically regarding finances. The most prevailing comment is that it is a reference to spiritual riches. The Thompson Chain Reference Bible is a wonderful resource and study bible, but at this point, he too in the margin describes what Paul is referring to as 'spiritual riches'; Jamieson, Fausset and Brown comes the closest saying, '…in the heavenly glory which constitutes His riches, and all other things, so far as is really good for us', Matthew Henry interprets it as, 'rich in the love of God, rich in the blessings of the new covenant, rich in the hopes of eternal life'. The Word Biblical Commentary, claiming a team of respected International scholars who were 'a showcase of the best in evangelical critical scholarship for a new generation', states regarding this verse; 'Here, surely wealth and poverty are ciphers, not for material prosperity and penury but for spiritual exchange as the Incarnate Christ became what we are, so we could become what He is'. For that to be consistent, the scripture would have to read, 'Christ… became (spiritually) poor, that you might become (spiritually) rich'. This then becomes an absurd, almost blasphemous proposition. To say or even intimate that Jesus Christ was a spiritually poor person is ludicrous. Here is a person who raised the dead, healed the sick, displayed complete prowess over demons and the devil, revealed the highest and deepest truths regarding God, man and the entire purpose of heaven that have withstood every kind of test and scrutiny. This person was not a spiritually poor person. Rather it was because of His spiritual richness that he was able to go to the cross and bear away the curses that afflict mankind. Even if we limit His poverty to the time He was on the cross, claiming it was our poverty that He took, are we to conclude that the 'hope' he entered into was a spiritually poor position? To maintain any kind of hope, and faith through His ordeal demonstrates an extraordinary spiritual richness. In our effort to read more into the statement than is actually there, we make fools of ourselves and prevent God fulfilling His great promises in our lives. Jesus became poor regarding the wealth of this world on the cross, that those who receive Him may become blessed with the wealth of this world.

Right at this point many people, (mostly Christians) have a terrible amount of trouble accepting that fact. The scheme of the devil has been to deceive the Church into believing that it is far more pious to be poor than it is to be rich. Suspicion is cast upon those who have accumulated wealth. God is seen as one who would rather his people be poor than enjoy abundance in their world. However, abundance has always been the will of God for His people.

Getting over a poverty mindset however, is a lot more difficult than most realize. A spirit of religiosity is at the root of this consciousness. Paul encountered it as early as the First Century when dealing with the errors of the Colossian church.

Colossians 2:18 Let no one cheat you of your reward, taking delight in false humility and worship of angels, intruding into those things which he has not seen, vainly puffed up by his fleshly mind,

The religious spirit enjoys being ascetic because it draws pride from the effort. This indulgence only actually severs a person from Christ. It is possible for people to be cheated out of what is rightfully theirs. Esau was cheated out of his inheritance because he valued a bowl of stew above his inheritance. The believer can also be cheated out of theirs because they simply don't value their inheritance above their appetites. Ascetism, (self inflicted austerity and poverty) is a different kind of appetite posing as spirituality and it cheats believers out of all the blessings Christ has won for them through the work of the cross. The thinking that says high spirituality is only gained at the expense of physical blessing defrauds the believer of their inheritance, whereas the Word causes us to gain it. Paul is referring to that Christianity that poses as 'humility'. This word is taken from Greek words translated *'depressed, humiliated in circumstances or disposition, not joyful but base, cast down, humble, of low degree and estate.*

We are called to humility, but not servility that embraces poverty and depression as though it were a form of piety that pleases the Father.

The other word this *'humility'* 'tapeinophrosune', is taken from is 'phren' meaning to rein in or curb the midriff (as a part of the body). That is figuratively speaking, reigning in the feelings, heart, the mind and understanding (cognitive abilities) as well. This then is saying that smallness, ('the reigning in') of feelings and mind is promoted by the religious spirit, again, as if this pleases God, but it actually cheats us out of our inheritance in Christ. The church has been notorious for thinking small, poor and backward, and then justifying all this because it is 'for the Lord'. This is intimating we do things small and second rate because it's for the Lord. This is ridiculous. God wants us to think bigger than we ever have before. We are not to limit God with our thinking, but release Him with ever increasing largeness and release, dreaming of great exploits for Him.

Right from the start those who have pleased God have enjoyed abundance in their lives.

Abraham became exceedingly prosperous as he obeyed God.

> *Genesis 13:2 Abram was very rich in livestock, in silver, and in gold.*

His son Isaac also prospered as the blessing of abundance promised Abraham also came upon his descendants.

> *Genesis 26:12 Then Isaac sowed in that land, and reaped in the same year a hundredfold; and the LORD blessed him.*
> *Genesis 26:13 The man began to prosper, and continued prospering until he became very prosperous;*
> *Genesis 26:14 for he had possessions of flocks and possessions of herds and a great number of servants. So the Philistines envied him.*

These people recognized the blessing of God was upon their lives because God had blessed them. The sons of Isaac were also blessed. As Jacob honored God in tithing as his grandfather Abraham had, he received a great abundance from the Lord.

Genesis 31:1 Now Jacob… has acquired all this wealth.'

Even Job who also lived round the time of Abraham was very wealthy. In fact he was considered to be the wealthiest man in the East.

Job 1:3 Also, his possessions were seven thousand sheep, three thousand camels, five hundred yoke of oxen, five hundred female donkeys, and a very large household, so that this man was the greatest of all the people of the East.

The devil had challenged the Lord that His servant Job only served God because he was blessed with abundance. The challenge was that if Job lost all his blessings he would forsake God. The challenge was that Job's blessings meant more to him than God did. The Lord believed that Job would remain true to the Lord, no matter what happened to him, whether he had nothing, or everything. The devil was granted permission to afflict the man with some of the worst sufferings we could read of, yet Job did remain true to the Lord. His wealth had not corrupted his soul, but rather had increased his sensitivity to the needs of those around him. He emerged from his nine month long trial victorious. He did not forsake God, and God rewarded him. The blessing of his latter years eclipsed all the blessings he had previously enjoyed.

Moses and Aaron received the tithes of all the priests who had received the tithes of all the people. (Numbers 18:28)

There were 600,000 men in Israel at that time. If we were to say two thirds of them were employed at $250 weekly, that's a $25 tithe multiplied by 400,000. That equals $10 million, the tithe of which is $1 million. This belonged to Moses and his brother. That adds up to about $52 million a year! This shows just how small our current day thinking is in this area. You would have to agree that the figures in these equations are conservative in today's world. Someone might say, 'But that was while they were wandering in the wilderness and they all had nothing much anyway. This is ridiculous thinking. They had literally plundered Egypt on the way out, and the laws Moses was instituting were designed for when they entered Canaan anyway. While this was meant to happen shortly after they had departed from Egypt, they were waylaid by their own unbelief at the sight of the giants. God had the largest people on Earth build the mightiest cities, plant the greatest farmlands in the best climate on the planet; all for His people Israel. All they had to do was go and take it. The only difficulty they would face was to oust the giants. God would be with them and the whole exercise was to be reasonably easy. However, they stumbled in their faith and wandered for forty years in the wilderness, not experiencing the abundance Yahweh had already prepared for them. This is much like the church in many areas today. We have seen giants in the land and been scared off from going in and taking what God has prepared for us. This life in Christ is meant to be an abundant one, at every level. We are not saved to become paupers in the Earth. Jesus died to set us free from poverty.

King David was also extraordinarily wealthy, so much so that he was able to give $2,835,000,000, (by today's conversion rates) i.e. $2.8 billion of gold over and above his regular offerings, for the building of the temple.

Twenty two times he refers to the offerings he brought into the House of God, his tithing, and the fulfillment of the pledges he had made to God. All this is part of the process by which the Lord brings blessing upon our lives.

King Solomon, the son of King David invited the Queen of Sheba to his palace. She was also extremely wealthy but was breath-taken at the expanse of the wealth of Solomon.

Even the prophets were not considered poor. Isaiah was considered to have come from a wealthy background, Jonah had enough money to purchase a ticket on a boat to a distant country, and Jeremiah was able to go out and buy an acreage for 17 shekels (about $9,000 - one shekel equaled 4 days wages) when the Lord told him to.

Jesus Himself received gold, frankincense and myrrh at his birth. From early antiquity it was diplomatically correct for kings to bring extravagant gifts to others kings, whether infant or grown, when they visited them for whatever reason.

We have texts from as far back as 1850 BC related to the Ancient Near East, from the city of Mari recording the vast inventories of gifts that were exchanged between kings of greater or lesser degrees when they were meeting each other. They reveal prodigious quantities of gold, ebony, and ivory, lapis lazuli, garments and sweet oil; sent in each direction as part of diplomatic protocol. Even though the amounts of these gifts add up to incredible sums, they pale in ordinariness compared to the first millennium BC practices. Osorkon (889 BC) gave gifts to Egypt totaling 445 metric tons of gold in the form of vessels, statues, furnishings and the like. Gifts came with the Queen of Sheba to the court of Solomon in an extraordinary abundance. However, the record tells us her breath was taken away at the grandeur of Solomon's obvious wealth. There are an abundance of records detailing what was considered diplomatically correct in the amounts of gift giving. In fact if a king's wealth was not represented in his gift, or the stature of the receiving King reflected sufficiently abundantly, the receiving king would let the giver understand in no uncertain terms that he had been slighted by the meanness of the gift.

The number of the Magi was not limited to three just because there were three categories of gifts mentioned in the Scripture. There were probably many more, and the gifts were not three single items of gold, frankincense and myrrh, but rather, these were the headings of inventories under which many different items would have been included. This was the norm for recording indexes of gifts for kings.

The wealth and influence of the Magi is clearly considerable because of the impact their coming had upon Herod.

This set Jesus up for life. The gifts were for Him, not His family, yet it would be reasonable to suggest that once He understood what his wealth was, He would have shared it with His earthly family.

During His ministry he was provided for by wealthy women who followed Him as he traveled.

Luke 8:3 and Joanna the wife of Chuza, Herod's steward, and Susanna, and many others who provided for Him from their substance.

These people were wealthy and there were many of them. They provided all of the Messiah's needs. Jesus' little band received so much that they needed a treasurer; Judas. It was at the cross that Jesus 'became poor'.

Paul traveled three times around the world, had enough to pay for a Roman trial, and was kept in prison for two years by the Roman procurator of Judea, Felix. The sole reason for his captivity was that Felix hoped for a bribe from the apostle. He would not have waited that long for a small amount. He knew Paul could deliver and waited for that.

Paul tells Philemon to put on his account anything the runaway slave Onesimus owed him. This could have been any amount. A slave owed his master a years wages for every day he was a runaway. Yet Paul was confident that he could pay. The Apostle supported an entire ministry team that traveled the world with him. As he labored at his craft he prospered because of the blessing God had placed on his life. (Acts 20:34).

Paul, who was a strict Pharisee, would have observed tithing as a regular practice all his life. He preached on giving abundantly, and also laying aside at the beginning of each week those first fruits of a person's prosperity. He fully accepted that Christians would prosper.

> *1 Corinthians 16:2 On the first day of the week let each one of you lay something aside, storing up as he may prosper.*

Those people who believe Christians should not prosper should get committed to being poor. If we are not meant to prosper, then it would be logical that God is wanting us poor and failing in life, so that we don't succeed and be prosperous at all. To believe that God does not will us to prosper, means we believe He does not want us to do well in life. He does not want us to be blessed with good things, with an abundance for our lives and those of others. If God wants His children to be poor (while He lives in the vast abundances and glories of Heaven), then we should certainly not be living in countries where the government will look after us in our poverty. We should be off to an undeveloped country, where we mark out a piece of the pavement for our home, or live in a cardboard box, and certainly not look for any wealth for medical needs or food. We should scavenge around rubbish tins looking for scraps of food along with all the other poor. This is what being poor is. If it is the will of God for us to be poor then should we not do it with all our might, become the very poorest of the poor? By now most say,

'Don't be ridiculous. We're not talking about *that* kind of poor. We should have enough to just get by moderately'.

'How much is moderate?'

'Just enough to get by'.

'For **who** to just get by?

You!

That has to be about the most selfish kind of Christianity ever postulated. How are you going to pay your neighbor's rent when they're out of a job? How will you be able to pick up a person who has been run over, robbed, beaten and left half dead on the side of the road? How will you be able to take them to the hospital and then offer to pay the bill for however long it takes them to heal?

Jesus said a true believer is someone who pays the price for the healing of the people who are wounded.

This is not talking about spiritual healing either. James says mere religious talk is futile (James 2:16). Real religion is when we physically help people. This is impossible without the means to do it. You cannot help people much when you have no means to help them. The Bible condemns the practice of simply sending your best wishes and statements like 'be warmed and filled' and do nothing to actually make that happen.

> *James 2:16 and one of you says to them, "Depart in peace, be warmed and filled," but you do not give them the things which are needed for the body, what does it profit?*

God wills that we enjoy an abundance in our lives so that we are able to assist others.

> *2 Corinthians 9:8 And God is able to make all grace abound toward you, that you, always having all*

sufficiency in all things, may have an abundance for every good work.

This is one of the largest and most wonderful Scriptures in the Bible. This says that God will cause an abundance to come into our lives, because of his grace towards us. Even though we don't deserve grace, even though we have done nothing to merit His favor, He has chosen to place this on our lives, and it manifests in abundance.

This is the will of God, that we enjoy an abundance not just on payday, not just when the tax refund comes through, not just when we get a bonus, not just when we receive an inheritance; but everyday, always. That means every single day of our lives. God is wanting us to enjoy a complete sufficiency in all things, so there is not one area we are insufficient in. But there's more! Paul goes on to declare that an abundance is decreed for our lives, so we can engage in every good work. We may think we're just going to get involved in giving to one missionary, or supporting a particular ministry, or to give to just one or two people who have needs. Yet the Lord wants us to have such an abundance that we can be a blessing to every good work. This is what the church is meant to be. We are meant to have such a prosperity in the church that we are able to supply the needs of those around us all of the time, in abundance.

17. WE HAVE HEALING

1 Peter 2:24 BY WHOSE STRIPES YOU WERE HEALED.

TLB 'For his wounds have healed ours!'

Jesus has taken our sicknesses upon Himself so that we do not have to bear them on ourselves;

> *'Matthew 8:17 He Himself took our infirmities And bore our sicknesses.*

This is the love of God in action. As a father of three children there have been times when each of them has been through tough times, emotionally, relationally, medically and circumstantially. There have been moments when I wish I could have switched places with them, knowing that I might have been able to bear it better after many more years of experience. Even when they have been ill, I have wished I could have their sickness so they would not have to bear it. This is what a father feels for his children, and what the love of God did for us and more! He *took* our sicknesses and made them His own, so we would not have to suffer.

If Jesus has borne our sicknesses then we no longer need to.

Healing is ours through the work of the cross. The Cross is the basis for wholeness. When Jesus took our sins away, He also took our diseases away.

Since the beginning of time, God has been the ultimate healer. When Jesus came into the world, it was in complete keeping with His Divine nature to heal sickness. It has always been the will of God to heal sickness. **Whenever God sees sickness, it's His nature to heal it.**

He revealed Himself as the healer of Israel through His name **Jehovah Rapha - 'The Lord who heals you' (Exodus 15:26).**

The Lord established the fact that if they serve Jehovah exclusively, then He would remove sickness from their lives.

> *Exodus 23:25 I will take sickness away from the midst of you.*

Throughout the Old Testament, time and time again, healing accompanies the **Atonement, Intercession** and the **Passover** sacrifices.

In **Genesis 20:17** Abraham intercedes for the women of the house of Abimilech. They are all healed.

When Israel left Egypt they sacrificed a lamb for each household. After this, there was **not one sick one** among them as they marched out of the land of their bondage. **(Psalm 105:37)**

When the Israelites were bitten by snakes in the desert, Moses lifted up a sculpted brass snake on a pole, and anyone who looked at it was healed **(Numbers 21:8,9).** Jesus Himself referred to this as being exactly what was to happen to Him **(John 3:14),** that He would be lifted up. Thus, it also follows, that whoever looks to the cross, just as the poisoned Israelites looked to a brass snake, they will discover healing.

In **Leviticus 14** we read of the priests placing the blood of a sacrifice on people diagnosed with leprosy. Once the ceremony was complete the leper was cleansed. Healing took place as the person received the blood of the sacrifice. Leprosy has always been a symbol of sin. The cleansing of the leprosy is a symbol of the cleansing of sin, plus it demonstrates actual healing of the disease as well.

When Hezekiah kept the Passover in 2 Chronicles 30:20, 'the LORD listened to Hezekiah and healed the people'.

In **1 Corinthians 11:30**, Paul tells the believers they are weak and sickly, because they have failed to correctly estimate the Lord's body. They did not grasp what Jesus had done for them through the cross.

All of these events tell us that healing and the atonement are connected.

Through the fall we lost everything. Through the Cross, Jesus recovered everything for us.

Salvation without sacrifice, without the shedding of blood, is unknown in Scripture.

Dr Young, author of Young's Analytical Concordance translates **Isaiah 53:4** as;

> *'Surely our sickness (Hebrew - 'choli') He has borne, And our pains He has carried them... And by His bruise there is healing for us'.*

Dr. Isaac Leeser, translator of the Hebrew English Bible, renders these verses as;

'He was despised and shunned by men; A man of pains and acquainted with disease. But only our diseases did He bear Himself, And our pains He carried'.

When Jesus was crucified He was dealing with more than just sin. He was providing the basis for healing, and delivering people from sickness. Many times the two actions are placed side by side. The Psalmist declares;

Psalm 103:3 (The Lord) who forgives all your iniquities, Who heals all your diseases.

In the forgiveness of sin there is also the healing of diseases. God is not limited to forgiving only a few select sins. He forgives ALL sins. The same applies to disease. He heals ALL diseases. There is no disease God is incapable of healing. Jesus saw little difference in setting a person free from their sin and setting them free from their sickness;

Mat 9:5 For which is easier, to say, 'Your sins are forgiven you,' or to say, 'Arise and walk'?
Mat 9:6 But that you may know that the Son of Man has power on earth to forgive sins'; then He said to the paralytic, 'Arise, take up your bed, and go to your house.'

The man was immediately healed. Jesus declared that healing and forgiveness of sin work together.

Faith makes real the promises of God.

To discover the power of the cross for healing I must know how to appropriate truth.

If it was a meal on a plate I could eat it.

If it was an item in a store I could purchase it.

If it was a fruit on a tree I could pluck it. Even though these may serve well as spiritual metaphors, the truth is we are always in need of knowing how to make invisible spiritual truths visible physical realities in our world. The bridge between the two is always faith.

Faith is speaking the Word and acting on it. Faith makes real the promises of God.

Faith is released because it is fully confident of the will of God.

If we are unsure of the will of God we will not have faith.

Healing has always been, is, and always will be the will of God. He never changes. **He's the same yesterday, today and forever. (Hebrews 13:8)** Jesus was the **express image** of God in the earth. **(Hebrews 1:3)** He is the perfect revelation of the will of God. He is the character of God manifested on planet Earth.

Not once do we find Jesus laying His hands on anyone to make them sick. The suggestion verges on blasphemy. He only ever healed the sick. Acts 10:38 tells us that it is the devil who damages people, and Jesus who makes them whole. When Jesus was asked if he would heal sick people, His answer was, **'Yes!' (Matthew 8:2,3).** He is no respecter of persons **(Acts 10:34).** What He has done for others, He will do for you and me. **All** who came to Him, He healed. **(Matthew 8:16)**

Few doubt Gods' ability to heal.

But many are uncertain of His willingness to heal **them.**

If He has healed others, why would He not heal you and me?

We are neither better nor worse than those God has already touched in other times. The precedent has been set!

God is no respecter of persons.

Faith always starts with **desire**. That means we want something to happen, badly. Faith wants a thing so much it will do whatever it takes to get it done. Faith begins with a desire that is so strong it makes you determined to make it happen. There is more.

Faith **decides** it **is** going to happen. Faith is determined. It has made it's mind up. Faith is not double minded. The decision is made. I'm going to get healed. I don't entertain 'But what if?' The decision is made. We're committed.

Faith **asks God** to make it happen. Faith cries out to God no matter what pressures there are to block us. Faith persists. It doesn't give up because of a few disappointments. It keeps on asking. It doesn't allow it's heart to be discouraged. Discouragement is amongst the worst enemies of faith. It is imperative to rise above every rejection and persevere until the answer comes.

Faith is **certain** of a miracle. It knows God is involved. It doesn't pretend. Faith is an inward clear knowing of realities that are not evident to the natural senses. Faith is so certain of those realities that it acts as though they are true; simply because they are. It makes decisions based on those certainties.

It plans according to what faith knows.

Faith **speaks** of those realities as finished acts. It says, 'Thank you Lord. It's already done'. 'It's already happened', 'I've got it right now', 'God has done it'. Faith always speaks. It's the first reaction faith has. If we believe a thing, we speak it. It's not necessarily loud, because it's not relying on volume, or excitement, but on the power of God's Word. Faith judges God as faithful. Faith speaks the promises of God and refuses to speak those things that oppose the promises. Faith acknowledges truth rather than facts. It connects the promises with the desires of the heart. Faith gives glory to God for things not yet manifested. Faith knows it first builds in the invisible world, then what has been formed in that realm manifests in the natural realm. Faith is a creative force, that's why it speaks in the same way God does when He creates. The Word of God and creative acts go together. He created the worlds through His Word. Speak the Word.

Faith **sees** realities not seen by natural eyes. It can see the healing already happened. It can **feel** the emotions of the experience, because it's there, in the future, in full view of the realities of the answer. Faith spends time meditating on that vision. Instead of imagining disaster, faith sees the answer.

Faith **acts**. Without action faith is dead. Real faith always acts. Faith does not care what obstacles there are. It will overcome them to receive the answer. Four men lift the roof to lower their friend into the presence of Jesus. The paralyzed man is healed. Bartimaeus, ignores the crowd trying to silence his cry for help. Jesus hears him, calls him and heals him. The

Canaanite woman pushes through the apparent reluctance of Jesus to heal her daughter. The disciples have driven her back, Jesus has first ignored her, then told her she doesn't qualify for a miracle, (she is a foreigner to Israel). However, the woman keeps coming in spite of all this. She gets the miracle.

In just the same way the Father has provided forgiveness for His children, so He has provided healing for all.

God has arranged for this healing to travel into our lives through different means. Even though God uses various ways to bring healing, it is always based on two things. The first is that healing has already been secured for us through the death of Christ on the cross. Secondly faith is always a part of the equation. Faith is the currency of heaven. Whether it is the faith of the person praying, the faith of the sufferer, or the faith expressed by others, releases the power of God that brings healing to sick people.

LAYING ON OF HANDS

Healing is imparted through the laying on of hands.

Mark 16:18 they will lay hands on the sick, and they will recover.

Through the laying on of hands the Spirit of God is imparted into people. Healing from God is a supernatural flow of the life of God. Healing is spiritual life. This 'life', is not nothing. We must understand that God is not nothing. God is something. God is spirit, and spirit is something.

John 4:24 God is Spirit.

God is actual. Spirit is not nothing. Spirit is something. Spirit is a substance albeit a spiritual one. Spirit substance cannot be seen with physical eyes, felt with our physical body, heard with physical ears, or smelled or tasted with our nose or mouth. Our physical bodies are not equipped to contact spiritual realms. Spirit relates to spirit. Flesh relates to flesh.

John 3:6 That which is born of the flesh is flesh, and that which is born of the Spirit is spirit.

Romans 8:5 For those who live according to the flesh set their minds on the things of the flesh, but those who live according to the Spirit, the things of the Spirit.

However, we are spiritual beings. Our spiritual nature finds expression **through** our physical bodies. We are 'temples' (1 Corinthians 3:16) of the Holy Spirit. Our own spirit lives within us (Daniel 7:15). The Father and Jesus dwell within us (John 14:23). These are all spirit entities. Spiritual life can be imparted from one person to another, from one thing to another. This happens through the laying on of hands. This applies to many more areas than just healing. However, healing is a primary application of the laying on of hands. The 'stuff' of God travels from one person to another through the laying on of hands. This 'stuff' can actually permeate physical things. Spiritual life can get inside physical things. Paul laid his hands on cloth and when it was placed upon sick people, whatever had gotten into the cloth was released into the sufferer's body, and they were healed.

Acts 19:12 so that even handkerchiefs or aprons were brought from his body to the sick, and the diseases left them and the evil spirits went out of them.

This miraculous power lives inside the physical body. We sometimes imagine that because spirit is not physical that it is somehow separate from our body. We can think we are a hollow case, and that our spirit dwells in the hollow. This is not the case at all. The spiritual life of God actually infuses the physical body. This life of God gets inside our flesh and our bones. This is where the healing life of God, the 'stuff' of God Himself lives.

Some time after Elisha, the miracle-working prophet, was dead and buried, groups of Moabite raiders invaded Israel. During one of the battles, Israeli soldiers were attempting to bury a comrade but the raiders attacked them. In their haste the soldiers threw the dead man into the tomb of Elisha. Before this, over time, the bones of the prophet had become exposed inside the tomb. As soon as the dead man landed on the bones of Elisha, he revived. He was resurrected by the power of God still resident in the bones of a dead man who once worked miracles through the healing power of God.

2 Kings 13:21 So it was, as they were burying a man, that suddenly they spied a band of raiders; and they put the man in the tomb of Elisha; and when the man was let down and touched the bones of Elisha, he revived and stood on his feet.

The power of God lives in our flesh and bones. It lives in

physical things. The presence of God permeates buildings and atmospheres. It infuses into our bodies, and our workplaces. This 'stuff' of God gets into things and works miracles, changing lives, healing sicknesses, and causing evil spirits to leave. It is the spirit of God. No evil spirit can remain as the power of God and the Holy Spirit take up residence. Light comes. Darkness goes.

This 'stuff' is imparted through the laying on hands. It travels from one person to another as we lay hands on people with that purpose in mind. It flows through the spiritual atmosphere of faith. It seems to matter little as to who actually is expressing that faith.

It can be the friends or relatives of a sufferer:

> *Matthew 9:2 Then behold, they brought to Him a paralytic lying on a bed. When Jesus saw their faith, He said to the paralytic, 'Son, be of good cheer; your sins are forgiven you.'*

> *Matthew 9:18 While He spoke these things to them, behold, a ruler came and worshiped Him, saying, 'My daughter has just died, but come and lay Your hand on her and she will live.'*

It can be the faith of the sufferer themselves;

> *Matthew 9:29 Then He touched their eyes, saying, 'According to your faith let it be to you.'*

It can be the faith of the minister for the healing;

> *Matthew 17:17 Then Jesus answered and said, 'O faithless and perverse generation, how long shall I be with you? How long shall I bear with you? Bring him here to Me.'*

If faith is absent and there is an active atmosphere of unbelief, this severely restricts the release and flow of this life of God. Even Jesus Himself was restricted by the unbelief of a cynical community.

> *Mark 6:5 Now He could do no mighty work there, except that He laid His hands on a few sick people and healed them.*
> *Mark 6:6 And He marveled because of their unbelief.*

—————— THE GIFT OF HEALING ——————

> *1 Corinthians 12:8 …to another (is given) gifts of healings by the same Spirit.*

Some people in the Church are especially gifted by the Holy Spirit to bring healing. They have a gift to heal sick people. All Christians can pray with an expectation for people to be healed (James 5:16), but there are definitely certain people gifted by God to minister healing to the sick. This gift is also their calling and motivation. They approach the entire Gospel from the aspect of healing. The revelation and insight these people have, travels down the line of healing sickness. Again this gift is generally imparted through the laying on of hands.

Because there are so many kinds of sicknesses it seems that God gives people giftings that heal certain diseases in particular. This arouses higher levels of faith for people with those particular sicknesses. 1 Corinthians 12:8 speaks of the healing gifts in plural terms.

PEOPLE ARE HEALED AS OTHERS JOIN TOGETHER AND PRAY FOR THEM

James 5:16 Confess your trespasses to one another, and pray for one another, that you may be healed. The effective, fervent prayer of a righteous man avails much.

When we pray for others we are interceding. We are standing in the gap. We are taking their problem on as though it was ours. We are standing before God on their behalf. Intercession gets results. As we pray fervently and effectively for one another, we bring healing to the church.

When I was a young assistant minister, a young boy suffering around 24 epileptic fits every day was brought to me. The parents expected healing. He was becoming cut, bruised and badly damaged. I felt so sorry for the kid and his parents, who were great people. The pressure on them was becoming unbearable. I took the matter to our mid-week meeting. We joined hands around the auditorium and began praying. A great spirit of prayer came upon us. We rose into a realm of prayer and intercession I have never experienced before. After a while it seemed we had prayed long enough. However, the Lord said to me, 'Rise again. You're not through yet'. So I told the people to rest for a few moments and then we would rise again in prayer. Again, after a while the stamina of the people began to flag. This was after about ten minutes of this kind of prayer. Intercessory prayer is very exacting. The spiritual stamina of most people in prayer is not great. Our spirit tires and we lose emotional and mental focus. I still felt we had not yet 'broken through'. We sang in worship, strengthening our spirit and then prayed a third time. This time we seemed to reach a crescendo and there was a definite 'crack' in the spirit. We broke through. People were clapping, shouting, jumping up and down. We had a deep witness something powerful had happened. I rang the parents of the young boy the next day. They told me he only had 4 fits that day. The next day he had none at all. Healing travels through prayer.

—— THE WORD OF GOD HEALS PEOPLE ——

Psalm 107:20 He sent His word and healed them.

In the Gospels often Jesus does not go to the sufferer, but rather simply speaks the Word and the miracle happens. (Matthew 8:4)

As people believe the Word, healing enters their lives, or to the one they are bringing to the Lord.

A friend of mine was diagnosed with cancer. It was about the size of an orange under his ribs and under his arm. His wife didn't allow anyone to speak anything negative anywhere in his room. She didn't allow anyone to visit him if she knew they were speaking negative things. They plastered the walls of his hospital room with Scripture, and began speaking the

Word of God day and night. When he was finally operated on, they found the cancer to be completely dead. Instead of him dying - the cancer did. Jesus lives, and so do those who believe Him. He heals. He works miracles. So do those who believe Him.

I have a list of Scriptures I often give people, called 'prescription promises'. The power of the Word of God is severely underestimated. The prophets Elijah and Elisha simply spoke the Word of God and each time, awesome miracles took place. Jesus spoke the Word time and again to impossible situations and miracles came to pass. Scripture carries healing and miracles into people's lives.

The Word of God is a miracle working healing force in the Earth;

> *Proverbs 4:22 For they are life to those who find them, And health to all their flesh.*

Revelation of the Word of God is the Word being revealed into our spirit. Revelation is light. It is truth entering our inner man. Revelation is the food of the spirit. Revelation of the Word of God is an actual life force that travels into our spirit and can be imparted through speaking it. The Word of God is a creative force. God created all that exists with His Word. The power of His Word has not been relaxed one iota. The same power is active in His Word now as was in His Word at the creation of the Earth and the entire Universe. When the Word enters our spirit, it comes as light. It is power that can be imparted. It is 'stuff', that can be sent into people's bodies and situations, and it brings miracles and solutions. It is the life of God.

18. WE HAVE THE HOLY SPIRIT

Ephesians 1:16-19 ...do not cease to give thanks for you, making mention of you in my prayers:
17 that the God of our Lord Jesus Christ, the Father of glory, may give to you the spirit of wisdom and revelation in the knowledge of Him,
18 the eyes of your understanding being enlightened; that you may know what is the hope of His calling, what are the riches of the glory of His inheritance in the saints,
19 and what is the exceeding greatness of His power toward us who believe...

Paul prays they will KNOW (grasp, embrace and experience) three things;

1. Destiny. They would understand their calling, individually and corporately. Every calling has hope... the anticipation of positive good in it. This is his first prayer.

2. Inheritance. He prays they would realise what are the riches of the glory of His inheritance in the saints.

3. Power. He prays they would fully grasp the exceeding greatness of His power toward those who believe.

We need revelation and insight from God because our natural mind does not grasp spiritual truth.

The Holy Spirit is given to us so we understand AND EXPERIENCE what God has given to us. In fact the word 'know' is most correctly translated 'experience'. The Holy Spirit comes to lead us into the experience of the inheritance.

> *1 Corinthians 2:12-14 Now we have received, not the spirit of the world, but the Spirit who is from God, THAT WE MIGHT KNOW THE THINGS that have been freely given to us by God.*
> *13 These things we also speak, not in words which man's wisdom teaches but which the Holy Spirit teaches, comparing spiritual things with spiritual.*
> *14 But the natural man does not receive the things of the Spirit of God, for they are foolishness to him; nor can he know them, because they are spiritually discerned.*

Adam Clarke Commentary: 'The spirit of a man knows the things of a man that is, a man is conscious of all the schemes, plans, and purposes, that pass in his own mind; and no man can know these things but himself. So, the Spirit of God, He whom we call the Third Person of the glorious TRINITY, knows all the counsels and determinations of the Supreme Being.'

Jesus told the disciples that when the Holy Spirit comes He would reveal truth to them.

> *John 16:13 However, when He, the Spirit of truth, has come, He will guide you into all truth; for He will not speak on His own authority, but whatever He hears He will speak; and He will tell you things to come.*

Jesus told the disciples that even though He was leaving He

was going to make sure that another, like Him would come in His place.

That person is the Holy Spirit, to continue to do all the things that Jesus Himself began.

The Baptism of the Holy Spirit is available for every believer;

> *Acts 2:39 For the promise is to you and to your children, and to all who are afar off, as many as the Lord our God will call.*

There is a difference between the Holy Spirit coming and residing within us and us receiving the clothing with power that Jesus spoke of - the baptism of the Holy Spirit. When the Spirit falls on our lives a brand new heavenly language is given to us.

All of us need to regularly be refilled with the Holy Spirit because we so easily slip back into operating in the natural man. The power of God seems to leak out of our lives, and we find ourselves struggling to keep walking with God.

We cannot afford to wander away from the Spirit. Christ did not perform one miracle until the Spirit had come upon Him. The world was 'without form and void' until the Spirit moved on the waters. The Church did not exist until the Spirit fell in the Upper Room upon the disciples.

John the Baptist said Christ will come and baptize His followers with the Holy Spirit;

The word baptism is an Anglicized word. This means that when it was translated into the English language from the Greek, it was basically left as it was. There were reasons surrounding this. The translators of the Bible were commissioned to do so by the King of England, King James I. The King of England was also the recognized head of the Church. This was a carry over from the days when the Church of England broke away from the Church of Rome. When the Pope refused to grant King Henry VIII a divorce, Henry decided that he would nationalize the church in his country. Thus began the Church of England.

In the Early Church people were baptized by full immersion. However, as time passed, for one reason or another, the practice of plunging new believers beneath the water passed away. Carrying out the ceremony only when the believer was of an age to understand what he was doing, also passed away. Babies were baptized as a matter of religious practice, if the parents were members of the Church. Neither did a person's spiritual state seem to matter. The ceremony was enough. In fact, the ceremony was seen as the process whereby the person became a Christian. Thus a person was thought to be on their way to heaven by virtue of his infant baptism.

This has always been the danger of religious 'acts'. Too easily they degenerate into heartless, empty, lip serving traditions. These are at best false securities. At worst they are vigorous enemies of God and His work in men's hearts.

So the practice became a ceremony of sprinkling with water for admission to the church. Derek Prince tells us that 'the relationship between James I and his bishops was not always too cordial. He did not wish the new translation of the Bible, published in his name and with his authority, to make his relationship with the bishops any worse. For this reason he allowed it to be understood that as far as possible, nothing was to be introduced into the translation which would cause unnecessary offence to the bishops or which would be too obviously contrary to the practices of the established church. Hence the Greek word 'baptizo' which could easily have become, in translation, a source of controversy, was never translated at all, but was simply written over in the English language.'

The word 'bapto' in Greek means 'to whelm, to cover wholly with a fluid'.

WHEN THE SPIRIT COMES

1.The Holy Spirit gives 'life' - He is called the 'Spirit of life'. The contrast between the giving of the law in the Old Testament and the giving of the Holy Spirit in the New is graphic, when we realise that when Moses descended from the mountain with the Ten Commandments, three thousand people died, yet when the Holy Spirit came down in the New Testament three thousand 'lived'. **The law of the Spirit of life sets us free from the law of sin and death**.

The key to living the way Jesus Christ wants us to is by being filled with the Holy Spirit. He is the enactment of the New Testament. The Old Testament was living by a set of rules. The New Testament is living by the Holy Spirit, who comes to live within you, and empower you to live according to the pattern He has written in Scripture. This is why it is so important to get filled with the Spirit, stay filled with the Holy Spirit and to live in such a way so we don't grieve or quench the Holy Spirit.

Dr. John G. Lake was a missionary to Africa many years before the modern Full Gospel movement. The deadly bubonic plague broke out in his area - hundreds died. He cared for the sick and buried the dead. Finally the British sent a ship with supplies and a corps of doctors. The doctors sent for Lake to come aboard and asked him, "What have you been using to protect yourself?" "Sirs," Lake replied, "I believe the law of the Spirit of life in Christ Jesus has set me free from the law of sin and death. And as long as I walk in the light of that law of life, no germ will attach itself to me." "Don't you think you had better use our preventatives?" the doctor urged.

"No," Lake said, "but doctor I think you would like to experiment with me. If you will go over to one of those dead people and take the foam that comes out of their lungs after death, then put it under the microscope you will see masses of living germs. You will find they are alive until a reasonable time after a man is dead. You can fill my hand with them and I will keep it under the microscope, and instead of these germs remaining alive, they will die instantly." The doctors agreed. They made the experiment and it was true. When they expressed wonder at what caused it Lake told them, "That is the law of the Spirit of life in Christ Jesus."

2. The Holy Spirit will empower you with 'dunamis' - the Greek word for power meaning supernatural ability. Divine energy. The Spirit of God came upon Samson and he became supernaturally strong; upon Elijah and he outran a chariot; upon Moses and he was able to deliver and govern an entire nation alone; upon 12 rough men, the disciples of Jesus, and they were able to turn the world upside own.

3. The Holy Spirit will place gifts within you. Some members of the family of God prophesy, some heal the sick. Every member of the Body of Christ is endowed with a supernatural ability from the Holy Spirit. No-one is without some ability from the Spirit to build the church.

4. The Holy Spirit will make you effective witnesses for Christ. Peter was transformed from a person embarrassed and fearful of being identified with Christ - to being the first to stand and fearlessly declare that Christ is Lord to the public. (Acts 2:14)

5. The Holy Spirit brings revelation of truth into your life as your teacher. The revelation of the truth of the Word brings the reality. As the Holy Spirit makes us aware of truth we are able to appropriate it, to apply it, to receive it, to experience it. That is why the Holy Spirit is given to us.

6. The Holy Spirit guides you in what you should do, and when and where you should go.

In 1849 Harriet Tubman, a Baltimore slave, escaped to Philadelphia and freedom. She returned in 1850 to guide her sister and two nieces to freedom, and then other relatives including her aged parents, and eventually between sixty and three hundred slaves. At one time, Southern reward for her capture stood at an astounding $40,000.

During the Civil War, (which she had foreseen in a vision

years earlier), she served both as a nurse and a northern spy and scout, securing military information from blacks behind Confederate lines.

Tubman, who was called 'the Moses of her people', 'never doubted' she was guided by God through dreams.

How do we receive the Holy Spirit?

> *John 7:37-39 On the last day, that great day of the feast, Jesus stood and cried out, saying, 'If anyone thirsts, let him come to Me and drink.*
> *38 'He who believes in Me, as the Scripture has said, out of his heart will flow rivers of living water.'*
> *39 But this He spoke concerning the Spirit, whom those believing in Him would receive; for the Holy Spirit was not yet given, because Jesus was not yet glorified.*

The first thing in receiving from God is to come to Him. He will not force Himself upon us. Come to him in prayer. Come to Him with your heart. Spend time drawing near to God. Secondly, get hungry for the Spirit. When you hunger and thirst for the Spirit He draws near. This is a desire that springs from a desperation for more of God.

There's the story of the old black preacher who was praying for a young man but the Holy Spirit wasn't coming. He took him to the river and held the boy under the water. The boy began struggling for breath, but the preacher held him under. He held him there until the boy exerted all his strength and overcame the downward push of the preacher. When he came up gasping for air the old-timer said to him, 'When you desire the Spirit like you desired air to breathe - just then, then you'll be filled with the Spirit!'

Thirdly the Spirit comes in many ways. Whatever way He comes receive Him. I remember a woman coming to us once to be prayed for to receive the Holy Spirit. She said she wanted the baptism of the Holy Spirit but not with tongues. We can't place conditions on how the Spirit comes. Let God be God. Let Him come, as He will. Generally there is always something about the way the Spirit comes that will be a challenge to us, however as we go with what He is doing we will find ourselves moving out of the natural into the spiritual.

Fourthly, act in faith. Many times people will say they can feel a language rising within them, but they feel it's just themselves. Of course it is. But it is also God. This is where faith comes in. We believe God is doing something. No one else is going to speak in tongues for us. We must do it, and it may feel somewhat unnatural to us. It will feel like it is us. The Holy Spirit does not overwhelm us so as to remove our capacity to control what's going on. As we co-operate with him, His power will come upon us in great measure.

Be filled with the Spirit!

CONCLUSION

What I'm about to say may come as a shock, but hear me out. Most of us think that when we pray and ask God to do something He will do it. But in the majority of cases this is not how prayer works. Our prayers bring God into what we do, rather than causing Him to do it Himself apart from our actions. The belief that God will answer our prayers independent from us, sets us up for regular disappointment. There are times when God will do things for us because there is no way we can do it ourselves. Yet what He is anticipating is that we will act, and the answer to our prayers will be God empowering us to fulfil what we set out to do.

God will not act independently of us.

When Jesus faced the tomb of Lazarus He told the people to roll away the stone. He will expect us to do what we can do and He will do what we cannot do. We can roll stones away. He can raise the dead.

When Jesus said 'I give you the keys of the Kingdom', that means He no longer has them. We do. When we act, those keys also become active. When we take up the authority, gifts and tools the Holy Spirit has imparted to us, power flows with us. Submitting ourselves to the will of God means we take action. It doesn't mean we sit back in a passive attitude. For many, this is all that submission means. However, submitting to the will of God is an aggressive position. Joshua did not stand on the wilderness side of Canaan and anticipate that God was going to conquer the land for them. They stepped out and God moved with them. They were successful in overwhelming the Canaanite hordes.

We set up strategies to win people to Christ and work hard at establishing them in church. As we do, God works with us and our efforts are blessed. We step out to plant churches. This takes enormous courage and resources. Sometimes we fail. However, as we persist, God works with us and we become successful. Even the failures turn around under the powerful redemptive processes of God. We step out to purchase properties. As we engage in the normal processes of business, God blesses our efforts and we prosper. We make investments to prosper in life. As we do God guides and we make wise decisions with investments, businesses and budgets. We seek connections with certain networks of people and God blesses our efforts. We seek to build teams and find ourselves with enormously successful people as we train and develop their lives.

Our attempts to succeed in life will be largely determined by our confidence. This rests on the way we see ourselves, what we believe about ourselves, what we believe we are capable of. Who we think we are and what we think we have is very often different to who we actually are and what we actually have. Bridging the gulf between the Word of God and our earthly realities is our life journey typified by the Israelites passage from Egypt into our promised land.

The way we see ourselves and the way God sees us is obviously very different. We may see ourselves as unsuccessful. He sees us as successful. He does not see us as losers, but as winners, high achievers, victors not victims. We may see ourselves as sick. He sees us healed. We may see ourselves poor. He sees us as blessed. We may think our lives are insignificant. He sees us as meaningful, impacting people. We may see ourselves falling short of His glory. He sees us as holy, irreproachable, justified and godly. We conform to the images we hold of ourselves.

As we gain a firm emotional and mental grip on the truth of the Word of God, our lives will be transformed, literally. We will morph into a brand new species of being, filled with the power of God. We will conform to the image God has of us, His image. God fills the new creation person with His great power. Today is the day to begin living the brand new life Jesus has given us. It's a choice we make, to live there. It's a fight we engage in to possess all that is ours. It's a journey from facts to truth, from the pages of the Bible to appropriated realities. It's the journey into our New Testament Canaan, escaping all kinds of bondage and entering into eternal freedom.

We must change our internal behaviour if we are to change our circumstances. If we will make changes to the way we think, the way we speak, the people we allow as influences, our mental and emotional diet, the habits we have, there is no doubt we can catapult ourselves into a far higher level of achievement than we've ever experienced.

Its important at this point to understand that all the ability we have is because we are 'in Christ'. John said 'without Him we can do nothing'. However Paul and other New Testament authors also write that 'with God nothing is impossible' and 'we can do all things through Christ who strengthens us'.

Whatever we can identify as lacking in our lives we can possess, simply through saying we have it. If you are impatient, say, 'I'm a patient person'. If you are a troubled person, say, 'I'm a peaceful person'. If you are sick, say, 'I'm healed'. If you are poor, say, 'I'm prosperous'. If you are weak, say, 'I'm strong'. If you are undisciplined, say, 'I'm disciplined'. If you are unwise, say, 'I'm wise'.

Then act like you are what you say you are. Don't just say these things. Live them. Start to walk, talk and behave like a strong person, like a disciplined person, like a prosperous person.

Make decisions today that take you into your promised land. It's yours. It's not just for everybody else. God has provided an amazing life for you. Jesus came to give you life, and life more abundantly. Take it today!

ACKNOWLEDGMENTS

Big thanks to my ever loving wife, Chris, who is not only a wonderful mother and nanna to our kids and theirs, she has managed to survive 44 years married to yours truly and bring many years of fruitful ministry at my side. Chris is my key proof reader for material such as this and brings a final polish to the script. Also thank you to my beautiful daughter Rebekah who I am deeply thankful for every day of our busy lives. I can't say how much I enjoy having her work along side us in a quest to build His church. Thanks Bek for producing such great work. A big thank you to Sasha of 'Mr & Mrs White' for bringing such style to our publications with her design and layout.

Thanks also to Kathryn Bourne, Tracy Akerman & Christina Burow for helping us with ideas and further proofing. Big thanks to Sumanth, our Indian colleague and friend doing such a fine job with our printing and delivery.

We are always better together.

If you enjoyed
THE BORN IDENTITY
we would like to recommend the following
books by Dr Phil Pringle.

Leadership Excellence

Keys to Financial Excellence

You the Leader

Moving In the Spirit

Hope

Parable of the Dog

Letters to Next Generation Leaders

Also by Chris Pringle.

Jesse – Found In Heaven

For more information please write to:

PaX Ministries Pty Ltd
Locked Bag 8, Dee Why NSW 2099 AUSTRALIA
Email: resources@philpringle.com

or visit the Phil Pringle website at
www.philpringle.com

LEADERSHIP EXCELLENCE

10 Characteristics Of Great Leaders will equip you with powerful tools to build and shape the leader in you. As founder and leader of the C3 Church movement, which consists of 300 churches worldwide, Ps. Phil's wisdom from years of consistency and fruitfulness fills this book.

KEYS TO FINANCIAL EXCELLENCE

This book is drawn from Ps. Phil's years of experience raising funds to build C3 church's impressive facilities at Oxford Falls and to support the movement's various ministries. Get insight into the principles used to build a highly diversified ministry training college, a primary and secondary school, an extensive church planting and missionary program and a weekly television show.

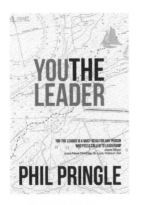

YOU THE LEADER

You the Leader is a 'must-read' for any person who feels called to Leadership in the body of Christ. The insight in this book, gained from over 30 years of pastoral ministry, is practical, biblically based, and includes thinking in the area of leadership that is revolutionary in today's contemporary church.

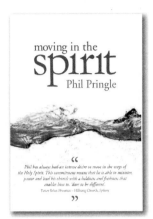

MOVING IN THE SPIRIT

Moving in the Spirit will guide and inspire you to tap into the great power of God and have it flow from you out into your world. You'll begin to not only know the truths of God, but personally experience them.

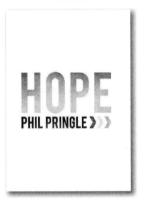

HOPE

The power of hope cannot be underestimated. Hope provides light in the darkness as well as maximizing the potential in every one if us. Like air, the positive expectation of good things is essential to the human race.

PARABLE OF THE DOG

Appearances can be deceptive. This is a small book with the cosiest of titles – The Parable of the Dog – and you might assume that it isn't deep. Presumably, Jesus' listeners felt the same when he started to tell parables of straying sons, mustard seeds or mugged Samaritans.

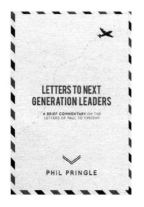

LETTERS TO NEXT GENERATION LEADERS

This translation of Paul the Apostle's letters to Timothy, will stretch your thinking and give you wisdom and proverbial insight into building the church of God in today's world.

JESSE - FOUND IN HEAVEN

"As I wept quietly, I had a very clear vision. I saw a young man laughing and walking".
Jesse - found in heaven, is Chris Pringles story, of a child lost by miscarriage and found again in God's hands through a remarkable vision.

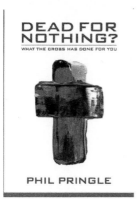

DEAD FOR NOTHING

The cross is central to our Christianity. Yet typically, the 'getting back to the cross' message is presented as a morbid, solemn experience of deep reflection, remorse and sorrow—but there is much more to the cross that we realise. The cross presents us with the singularly most powerful and enormous work of God in the earth.